Those Things We Treasure

Those Things We Treasure

A Selection of Speeches on Freedom and in Defence of Our Parliamentary Heritage.

The Right Honourable
JOHN G. DIEFENBAKER

Macmillan of Canada
Toronto

ISBN 0-7705-0957-6

Printed in Canada
by Ronalds-Federated
for The Macmillan Company
of Canada Ltd.,
70 Bond Street, Toronto.

Contents

Introduction

by
B. T. RICHARDSON

The critical issues of human affairs come into
sharp focus through long and often acri-
monious debate, from which truth emerges as
self-evident affirmation. In the example of
Canada, such an affirmation was the decision
to confederate in the nineteenth century. It was
reached after long years of debate and experi-
mentation and it was incorporated in the terms
of Confederation finally established in 1867.

The concept of Canadian Confederation
turned out to be surprisingly flexible and adap-
table, giving assurance of national survival in
following years of unimagined social and
economic change. The process of debate,
meanwhile, has remained incessant, adding to
the body of wisdom which serves to guide the
thinking of the Canadian people about the
course of national development. The process
has, as well, enabled Canadians to reject error
leading to ultimate disaster.

A free nation's decisions are often embodied in a series of events or, less frequently, in a single declaration. The vision to sum up and reconcile a nation's differences is not often possessed by a statesman, as it was in the case of President Abraham Lincoln's Second Inaugural address which conciliated the mood of the American Republic in the midst of its bitter civil war.

In an earlier republic, the Roman orator Cicero chose the Senate as the forum in which to expose the dangers that threatened the community and to give utterance to the verities that took possession of the conscience of citizens. Cicero's warning against the Catiline conspiracy survives as an unmatched oratorical statement in defence of the Roman Republic against tyranny and dictatorship. He defended and upheld the ethical standards of Roman life.

Simmering controversy over the future constitutional design of Canada has centred upon engendered issues such as the forms of monarchy and the structure of Parliament. In this selection from his speeches, Canada's great parliamentarian, the Rt. Hon. John G. Diefenbaker, discusses the present attack upon the parliamentary system of Canada, which consists of the Crown, the federal Parliament, and the Provinces. No Canadian speaks with greater understanding or broader experience of Parliament than does the former Prime

Minister. He traces the origins of Canadian liberty, which are the same origins from which freedoms developed for other nations as well. The book includes in text some of his earlier speeches relevant to the functioning of Parliament, the orientation of public policy and the preservation of liberty in Canada.

The texts include Mr. Diefenbaker's speech to the 1967 Centennial Convention of the Progressive Conservative Party — *One Canada, One Nation*. His famous address to the United Nations General Assembly, in which he called on Soviet Russia to grant to its captive nations the right of self-determination is also included, as well as his speech on the occasion, in 1963, when he was given the Honourary Freedom of the City of London.

This book is unique in the Canadian record both as a penetrating analysis of the recent drift of Canadian affairs and as a warning of dangers to be avoided if the Canada erected by the Fathers of Confederation is to survive. It is a re-affirmation of the truths upon which the Canadian nation was founded. It is strictly within the Canadian context, as President Lincoln's re-affirmation of the verities of the American Republic occupied the American context. It is a statement of views by a law-learned political leader and the acknowledged defender of Canadian liberty, the author of the Bill of Rights in Canada.

The days may not be as dark for Canadians today as they were for Americans in Lincoln's time, or for the Romans of the age of Cicero when their early republic was crumbling. Yet it is a time for Canadians to add to the documents of their liberty and the foundations of their future. In uncertain and clouded times, John Milton grasped his pen to write the finest statement of English liberty, designating his essay "Areopagitica" in reference to the hill of Ares where the highest judicial court of ancient Athens convened. It is a time for Canadians to document the vision of an enduring nation enjoying imperishable freedom that moved the Canadian colonists more than a century ago in the conferences at Charlottetown and at Quebec.

John Diefenbaker speaks to Canadians from Parliament Hill. In this book he writes of the constitutional organization of the Canadian nation and the foundations of Canadian freedom that must be preserved.

1

Parliament
Under Attack

"The present Parliament is like a cemetery in which only the dead have been left to guard it."

Canadians share in an imperishable political tradition which is British in its origins and which has been adopted and adapted by peoples around the world, notably the nations of the Commonwealth and the American Union. Much has been written as, generation after generation, men have examined the values inherent in this tradition and reaffirmed their acceptance of it. Such an examination is under way in Canada at the present time, not because of any ostensible breakdown in the constitutional framework of the Canadian nation but because of a series of overt criticisms by certain holders of high office whose apparent tendencies are to disregard and bypass certain traditional procedures.

One must remember that it was Prime Minister Trudeau himself who raised doubts about the parliamentary system of government in his first speech after he was elevated to the position of Prime Minister. That was on September 16, 1968, when he referred to "pride in this historic institution" of Parliament, and then added qualifications such as "whether our systems of government have outlived their effectiveness", and "whether new approaches and new institutions are necessary". He then asserted that "the institutions of government are not reflective of the demands of 1968". He asserted that "the traditional techniques of government are incapable of responding adequately and in time to the changing needs of society".

Mr. Trudeau's attitude to Parliament as an institution was expressed clearly by him on July 25, 1969, when he said: "The Opposition seems to think it has nothing else to do but talk ... The best place in which to talk, if they want a forum, is of course Parliament. When they get home, when they get out of Parliament, when they are fifty yards from Parliament Hill they are no longer members—they are just nobodies."

What is the alternative to the institution of Parliament? An authoritarian regime? Government by ministerial directives? Cabinet decisions and a three-day parliamentary session to give the stamp of approval? When he was Liberal House Leader, the Hon. Donald Mac-Donald remarked: "There is accumulating evidence to suggest that the parliamentary system simply cannot handle the growing work load of modern government."

In my view, the 1960s witnessed the decline of Parliament; the 1970s will see it become totally ineffective unless the public takes notice of what is happening and exerts the pressure of public opinion to preserve historic Canadian liberties and the institution of Parliament.

Parliament, in my view, is equal to the task. If the work load is heavy, the daily hours of sitting may be extended. Overtime would not create a precedent. It has been used before and can be used again, to whittle down a backlog of bills. The basic feature of Parliament that should not be impaired in any way is that it is, as the English authority, Bernard Crick, has put it, "a form of publicity." Controversial bills need to be debated at length so that the public is fully informed. "Its real functions," said Professor Crick, "are those of alerting and informing the public on matters relevant to the decision which way (or whether) to vote."

I have warned that in recent years Parliament is becoming a declining and dwindling institution. Effective debating has ceased, though debates in the House of Commons should serve as nothing else does to inform the public about the public's business. Parliamentary debate is one of the basic safeguards of freedom, and when it is curbed freedom is without defence. Writing in 1972 of Parliament as it is being conducted, one notes many occasions on which ministers have given misleading answers, thereby exhibiting their contempt for Parliament; they then rush out and doctor up their answers for the Canadian people. What a travesty! Ministers make important statements outside the House of Commons, following a course of "rule by news releases", thus making the chamber a caricature of Parliament. Speeches are read *ad nauseam,* and now it is proposed to table speeches without even bothering to read them. That is precisely the practice that has destroyed effective discussion in the United States House of Representatives. The present Parliament is like a cemetery in which only the dead have been left to guard it. This is the Parliament in which at the outset, the Prime Minister offered this veiled threat, to which I supply italics: "We are given an opportunity in this place, in this session, *which may not again present itself,* to prove to Canadians, ourselves included, that a Parliamentary form of government is not only capable of meeting the demands of this complex age, but that it is more capable of doing so than is any other form."

The Role of Opposition

Only a strong and alert Opposition can hope to check and control the excessive powers, contrary to the constitution, that may be assumed or conferred upon governmental administration, the so-called bureaucracy. Only an alert Opposition can prevent the short cuts through democratic procedures that cabinet ministers and bureaucrats frequently find attractive. It is only the Opposition, functioning as a recognized part of parliamentary proceedings, that stands opposed to the degeneration of the governmental system into a form of arbitrary direction of public affairs by the executive and the bureaucracy. Without it minorities would stand unprotected. Freedom would wither, individual liberty would be in jeopardy. Unwarranted and oppressive invasion of private rights would grow unchecked.

Without an effective Opposition, the administration in office could and would carry on the task of running the country, under circumstances identical with a totalitarian one-party state. To some this may seem an efficient way of running the country, but the first victim under such a regime—as Hitler, Stalin and Mussolini demonstrated—is freedom itself. Without an Opposition, it is not too much to say, the parliamentary system of government would fail in its primary task of protecting the rights of individuals and minorities, and of ensuring freedom and democracy.

In the parliamentary system, an Opposition is as necessary as the Cabinet itself. One without the other would mean tyranny or chaos. It is commonplace that governments view an effective Opposition as an obstruction. This is a view that is, too often and too lightly, taken up by unthinking critics outside of Parliament. An Opposition that discharges its parliamentary responsibilities may appear, in the superficial view, to be obstructionist. Extended opposition means lengthy debate. It was the British Labour Party chairman, Professor Harold J. Laski, who wrote that "the alternative to the 'talking shop' is the concentration camp."

Attacks on the Monarchy

In much the same fundamental way, constitutional monarchy serves to protect freedom and democracy against excessive and onerous political power. When the death was announced of Field Marshal Lord Alexander, a former Governor General of Canada, the Trudeau government defied tradition and the protocol that the Canadian flag on the Parliament Buildings should be lowered to half mast. This incident betrays a deep-seated hostility to the Canadian monarchy, based on ignorance of the measure of liberty and democracy represented in our system. Constitutional monarchy, which has taken many years to develop despite mistakes and missteps, is essentially a cure for excessive and tyrannical exercise of power at the apex of the parliamentary democracy of Canada.

Examples of the ascent of private individuals to high office leading to the uncontrolled exercise of power hardly need be given. The political systems of the world contain many examples. The constitutional problem is to prevent the transformation of elected representatives into tyrants and dictators. Our constitutional monarchy is based upon a separation of function between the representative of the Crown, who has no power but remains permanently in office at the summit, and the elected head of government who advises the Crown, exercises power and is subject to electoral defeat and to the necessity of regular elections.

Writing of this system, Dr. Frank MacKinnon noted, in the *Dalhousie Review:*

> The Monarchy therefore serves democracy. It keeps the ministers in second place as servants of the state—electable, responsible, accountable, criticizable, and

defeatable—a position necessary to the operation of parliamentary government. The people and their Parliament can control the head of government because he cannot identify himself with the state or confuse loyalty to himself with allegiance to the state and criticism with treason. He is discouraged from the common tendency of officials, whether elected or not, to regard and make themselves indispensable, to entrench themselves in expanding power structures, to resent accountability and criticism, and to scoff at the effects of prolonged tenure of office or advancing years. Moreover, such control avoids the charges of treason, executions, assassinations, revolutions, and miscellaneous other expensive upheavals which so often accompany attempts to control and change governments that take themselves too seriously.

In short, the opportunity to criticize and remove governments exists in a constitutional monarchy and it is, therefore, a system that works better than others, especially than those which must rely at times on assassinations and other violent forms of change. It contains the cure for a self-perpetuating elite, when government tends to rely on charisma and propaganda rather than on well defined and well controlled and fully accountable responsibilities.

There are other arguments for a constitu-

9

tional monarchy, as Dr. MacKinnon pointed out. The monarchy encourages dignity and respect for government. It furnishes the opportunity for a royal family to set an example. It admits pageantry to the process of government, and the sponsorship of good works and the inevitable social activities associated with government. It may be a source of honours and awards and of the unifying force that is desirable among a free people, and a continuing focus for loyalty and emotion. There is no competition between the monarch and the prime minister, such as one finds frequently in the operations of a system which has an elected president and an elected prime minister as well. An elected president operates within an entirely different system of government. He could not function within a system of parliamentary democracy such as Canada enjoys.

No system can guarantee good government as such. But the constitutional monarchy does guarantee that governments are responsible and disposable, and this allows smooth transitions from one political party to another, as the voters may determine.

Canadians [Dr. MacKinnon writes] have retained the Crown as represented by the Sovereign, the Governor General and the Lieutenant-Governors. All the reasons for the Crown have applied in both federal and provincial governments, and, on the whole, the relations between the Crown and the Ministers have worked extremely well. The twelve incumbents together cost a little more than two cents per citizen per year. By no stretch of the imagination can Governors General or the Lieutenant-Governors be considered to have played any significant role in actual government in our time, or to have obstructed or overshadowed their Premiers. Their job has been to occupy the top levels in their respective jurisdictions and to handle the decorative and emergency functions, while leaving the Prime Ministers and Premiers to handle the powers of government without actually possessing them, and to be electable, responsible, accountable, criticizable, and removable.

Origins of Our System

It is of interest to take note of the historical origins of the system of constitutional government under a monarchy, and the necessities that have given rise to such a system. It was in the British Isles that this system evolved and one of the most obvious characteristics of the population of those islands for centuries has been its blend of many racial stocks—the Jutes, the Angles and Saxons, the Picts and Scots and Celts, the Danes, and the Normans. The small British Isles have known the greatest assimilation in all history, of blood and brains and brawn. St. George, the lasting symbol of the English genius for assimilation, was the Greek son of a Christian governor of Palestine in the days of the Emperor Diocletian. He laid down his life rather than renounce his faith. He slew the dragon to save a maiden in distress. As the *Anglo-Saxon Chronicle* noted: "The blessed George was high in despising low things."

Those who have sprung from England have reason to be proud that never in history has such a small population, occupying so small an area, exercised so much influence over so many centuries. Indeed, the pages of history record the wreckage of those nations which disdainfully failed to recognize or understand this fact of history. England is a paradox of ancient traditions and wise democracy. Entering Westminster Hall I am always greatly moved by the knowledge that it is the place where the first true Parliament was convened by Simon de Montfort, and where Charles I was tried for treason, and where the trial of Warren Hastings was carried on for seven years.

An example of changelessness took place at the end of World War II when repairs were to be made to St. Stephen's Chapel. A Committee of Parliament was formed and a delegation went to Shropshire in search of the staunchest oak. They found the oak tree they needed and went to the Lord of the Manor to inquire if they might have it. He replied: "The answer, I fear, is 'No'—just as it was the last time some chaps from parliament wanted to make off with it." "When was that?" asked the chairman. "1348", replied the Lord of the Manor.

The British political legacy, which the United States shares with the nations of the Commonwealth, places emphasis on: (1) the dignity and worth of the individual citizen, regardless of his calling, his race, or his creed; (2) a passionate concern for individual liberty, tempered by a sense of social responsibility; and (3) the supremacy of the rule of law in the sense that every person, be he governor or governed, is subject to the law.

The English have evolved institutions whose reality is founded on the strength of the spirit, in harmony with eternal truths that have stood the test of time. They have shown an instinctive political genius to adopt, adapt, and develop the institutions of government, and have changed and altered them to meet the needs of the many races of people who have come under their influence.

The genius of British political institutions is that they have maintained tradition with the necessary flexibility. Magna Carta and other charters of freedom, and Parliament itself, though nurtured in English soil, have matured when their seeds have been planted in the far corners of the earth. They have grown and adapted themselves to meet the needs of countries and peoples and races everywhere in the world. In this process of adoption and adaptation, Canada was the first among the nations in the British Empire or Commonwealth to have religious freedom; the first to abolish slavery; first to have responsible government; first to bring about the establishment of free and independent nationhood while maintaining a democratic monarchy.

The parliamentary system that Canada inherited and that Canadians have caused to flourish in a new environment is not something to tinker with lightly, or to lay aside thoughtlessly.

2

The Twilight of Liberty

"What is being done by the Trudeau Government could be summed up in the words of Sukarno as 'guided democracy', in which freedom of the individual is diminished and the power of the governing authority is multiplied."

Millions of Canadians are concerned because the monarchy is being undermined, and some of the reasons for that concern should not be forgotten. In December 1968, *Time* magazine said that at the Government caucus, discussion had taken place at which the Prime Minister said:

> The government hopes to "Canadianize" the monarchy by quietly "depersonalizing" the Queen's role in favour of more emphasis on the constitutional position of the Governor General—by, for example, replacing the name of the Queen with that of the Governor General on all official documents.

The Crown is an integral part of Parliament which consists of the Queen, the Senate, and the House of Commons. Changes in the British North America Act cannot be made except by an amendment. What was being done was to amend it surreptitiously by governmental action without parliamentary assent.

In the Speech from the Throne in 1969, the following words, written by the Prime Minister, were spoken by the Governor General: "May I say, too, that Her Majesty's interest in Canada and in Canadians and their affairs will bring the

Queen. . . ." It is colossal effrontery to use these words, "Her Majesty's interest in Canada", when she is part of Parliament.

The B.N.A. Act states in Section 17: "There shall be one Parliament for Canada, consisting of the Queen, an Upper House styled the Senate, and the House of Commons". I should add that all reference to the Queen had been omitted in the 1968 Speech from the Throne and I raised objection thereto.

Throughout the years at all times in the Speech from the Throne the appropriate wording when legislation is to be introduced has been: "My Government will bring before Parliament . . ." These words "My Government" were entirely omitted in the Second Session of 1968, although they had been used in the first session in that year.

Other examples of the trend to tamper with our traditional heritage and remove it may be noted.

Unification of the armed forces (which resulted in a serious decline in morale in the forces) appears to have had among others the purpose of getting rid of the designation "Royal", and to eliminate the uniform worn by members of the armed forces, which bore a similarity to British uniforms.

The abolition has been carried out of the Canadian Guards, who were Her Majesty's Guards.

17

The Queen's portrait was removed from the Citizenship Courts until I raised strong objection, whereupon the portrait was replaced in some though not all of the courts.

A ban has been put into effect on Canadians receiving military decorations that originate in the United Kingdom.

Three Ministers of the present Government have stated their support for a republican system, and their view is reflected in steps to turn Parliament into a kind of Congress.

I have set out but a few illustrations of the trend that is taking place, which leads to the unanswerable conclusion that our traditional heritage is being whittled away and eroded, with the purpose in mind of establishing a republican form of government.

The Languages Issue

In the light of these tendencies, the preservation of the constitution becomes a primary concern. The search for methods of amending the constitution has, in Canada's case, been particularly arduous. I believe that search must not be abandoned, and the temptation to bypass the constitution must be resisted at all times. A disturbing example of yielding to such temptation is found in the experience of the Pearson Government in relation to language rights, which have become a focus of friction among Canadians. Let me examine this situation briefly, and propose a remedy.

Language rights in Canada rest upon constitutional provisions written into the British North America Act. The constitution was bypassed and changed without constitutional amendment, by the extension of language rights by means other than a constitutional amendment. Mr. Justice Thorson, a former Minister in the Mackenzie King government and subsequently President of the Exchequer Court of Canada, after his retirement from the bench, and as a private citizen, attempted to bring an action in the Supreme Court of Canada challenging the Official Languages Act on constitutional grounds. The Supreme Court refused to hear the action. The courts are being denied the right to determine whether what was done was within the powers of Parliament. The Pearson and the Trudeau governments have stored up much trouble for the future in their handling of languages rights.

I recommend, as a course of action to mitigate such a threat to Canada's future, that the device of a dominion-provincial conference be utilized to clear away the threatened troubles. I recommended such a course to Parliament on February 4, 1963, but an election leading to the defeat of the government of that day intervened. The Pearson Government relied on the instrument of a Royal Commission on Bilingualism and Biculturalism. The harvest of trouble that ensued from that policy is still with us, and it is plainly increasing as the days go by. I voted against the legislation on language rights based on the recommendations of the Bi and Bi commission, and I believe that steps must be taken to rectify the error resulting from a flagrant attempt to evade and bypass the constitution.

In view of the turmoil that flowed from mistaken initiatives taken by my successors, I believe that my proposal was correct. The deep shadow that lies across relations between the central government and the provinces as a result of the federal initiative in legislating in this field without proper consultation with the provinces, must be lifted. A way must be found to overcome the areas of disagreement that have been intensified rather than meliorated.

Sharp differences have arisen in the country over language rights, but I assure my readers that an alternative exists. The time for conciliation and an end of dissension has arrived. The alternative is that which we proposed in 1963. I recall my proposal to Parliament at that time, in words recorded in Hansard. I said:

> Confederation was achieved by a partnership of English-speaking and French-speaking men who believed that the destiny of the north half of this continent might be achieved in unity but not in uniformity. But for the fundamental agreements expressed in section 133 of the British North America Act, with its assurance of the rights of language in this country, and sections 91 and 92 assured to the provinces their jurisdiction over education and culture, there never would have been a Canada. The recognition of the two cultures and of the English and French languages was the very base and foundation of Confederation.

I proposed that a dominion-provincial conference "of the fullest breadth" be called. It would study such issues as the patriation of the constitution and adequate representation in the public service. It would consider the choice of a national flag and other symbols of Canadian sovereignty. It would, I said, "examine biculturalism and bilingualism in a comprehensive manner." I went on:

> The conference will provide the opportunities to examine areas of disagreement

and the nature of the courses of action required to resolve them. It will be intended to contribute to unity, harmony and a restatement of the goals of the Canadian Confederation. It will not be its purpose to seek uniformity in a country which has chosen unity in diversity, not unity through uniformity. In correcting any injustices that might be found we shall destroy prejudice and misunderstanding. We are ready to take action to deal firmly and positively with any danger which confronts the basis of the Canadian Confederation.

Canadians must continue to offer to the world the example of a nation composed of peoples who, though differing in language, culture and traditions, hold before mankind the beacon lights of mutual understanding and mutual respect. To the original French and English strains in the Canadian population there have now been added many Canadians of other origins. They have come of their own choice to this country and have become members of the Canadian family, bringing with them their traditions and rich heritages of culture. By their contributions they have enriched, deepened and diversified the cultures of this nation.

I see the Canada of tomorrow, Mr. Speaker, stronger, more united in her diversity, drawing her strength from the partnership of the two great original cultures and enriched by the infusion of many other races and cultures. Such a Canada is destined to play an ever greater and beneficent role in the world as an example of cultures and peoples abiding together in unity.

Language is an attribute of freedom and of sovereignty and we should always remember that the Canadian Confederation is based upon language rights specified in the constitution. Any attempt to "oppress the one language or to render it inferior to the other", as Sir John A. Macdonald said, would be impossible if it were tried, and foolish and wicked if it were possible.

Alienation of Canadians

I have never seen such widespread alienation as there is across this country today. The fear and frustration of many of our citizens is developing into a spirit of defeatism. The youth of Canada are desperately seeking ways in which they can influence the course of events. No leadership comes from the present Government in quality or direction. What sense of purpose can be derived from those who should inspire the aspirations of the people, but instead weaken the spirit through legislation that dwarfs the higher values that any great nation must have?

Those who believe in the principles that made this nation great will not be deluded by propaganda which appears to assert that the history of this country began on June 25, 1968. The values that inspire this country must not be lost by default by those who would tinker with Canada's destiny.

When I was Prime Minister I had the privilege of leading a Government that brought together the hearts and souls of Canadians through the National Development Policy. I said, in effect, "Let us go to work for Canada." Today there is one four-letter word that is not used by those who advocate change through revolution—*work*.

The World Scene

Internationally Canada has lost prestige under the Trudeau Government.

In the Commonwealth there has been a distinct breaking away under this Government from our normal relationship which has prevailed through the years. Indeed, at the Prime Ministers' Conference in London, the British press was shocked at the failure of Canada to make any serious contribution and to take any normal interest in the preservation of this great world company of peoples owing allegiance to the Queen, either as Sovereign or Head of the Commonwealth.

Canada is being taken, in other freedom-loving countries, to be a neutralist country. Canada's decision to reduce its connection with NATO has given a feeling of deep concern to the NATO countries.

The international situation today reveals a degree of unsettlement in the minds of men, coupled with the fear of another world war, which has not been equalled in intensity in my lifetime. The failure of the United Nations to carry out the basic principles of the Charter, and the continuing conduct of the Big Powers in evading and avoiding having matters of importance to them settled in the United Nations, have emasculated that world institution.

In recent years I have visited the U.S.S.R. and some Western European countries, as well as Japan, Taiwan, and South Vietnam, and everywhere men are fearful of the morrow. The U.S.S.R. and Mainland China are engaged in a world-wide effort to destroy freedom and in competition for the hearts of men everywhere in the world, although each of these powerful nations fears the other.

When he was Secretary of the United Nations, U Thant warned repeatedly of the danger of another world war, but his warnings have been unheeded. An imperative need of an effective international peace-keeping force under the aegis of the United Nations has been side-tracked because the major powers will neither give effective support to such a force nor provide for a contribution of their nations to such a force. The U.N. has failed to pass a Charter of Human Rights and Fundamental Freedoms to take the place effectively of the Declaration of Human Rights. The Declaration, while magnificent in its idealism, is totally ineffective in preventing the abuse and degradation of human rights by the U.S.S.R. If there had been a Charter of Human Rights, what has happened to the captive peoples of the Ukraine, the Baltic States, and other nations in the world could have long since been remedied by international action.

As I view the critical situation in which the

United Nations finds itself I believe that for the U.N. to survive: (1) there should be a rewriting of the Charter, which is out of date in many ways; (2) a United Nations Charter of Human Rights must be brought into being; (3) the International Court of Justice must be given compulsory jurisdiction.

As it is today, the Court's jurisdiction rests in the main on agreement with the alleged national wrongdoer in each case that the Court's adjudication will be accepted. Today, if the U.S.S.R. destroys the rights and fundamental freedoms of captive nations, there is no jurisdiction in the Court to protect the victims, without the consent of the U.S.S.R.

Canada, a number of years ago, accepted compulsory jurisdiction of the Court and as well, while exempting therefrom matters of a domestic nature, left it for the Court and not Canada to decide whether the matters in issue before the Court are of a domestic nature. It would strengthen the World Court if the nations would agree on compulsory jurisdiction of the Court, except in a matter of a domestic nature as determined by the Court.

The U.S.S.R. pretends at the United Nations to be the leader in support of the rights of emerging peoples, despite the fact that in the U.S.S.R. there is no freedom of speech or of the press, or any genuine freedom of religion and conscience. The intellectuals and writers are

27

tried behind closed doors and today are being imprisoned because they have exercised rights which are recognized by the Universal Declaration of Human Rights.

In 1960 at the United Nations I called upon the U.S.S.R. to live up to the principle of self-determination of subject peoples as it had undertaken to do under the Charter. I spoke out against the perfidy being practised by the U.S.S.R. against the Ukraine, the Baltic States, and other captive nations in refusing these nations the rights of self-determination through free elections. It was the first time that this had been done and it has been said that there was a considerable improvement in the treatment given to captive nations of the U.S.S.R. in the days and months immediately following the 1960 session of the United Nations and since.

No one in his right mind would suggest war as a means to free captive nations, but I am convinced that if the Western nations were to speak out, year by year, in the United Nations, against the double-tongued hypocrisy of the U.S.S.R. which condemns other nations for colonialism and at the same time denies self-determination to nations under its domination, self-determination of captives would by force of world opinion be brought about.

Canada's representatives to the United Nations have not spoken out since 1963. Why the muteness and silence on a matter that affects

120 million people in Europe and Asia? Some claim it would cause division in the United Nations. Is there to be one rule for the U.S.S.R. and its satellites and another for the representatives of the free nations? The Soviet representatives express their criticisms against the free world without hesitation in the United Nations. Why should not Canada and other freedom-loving nations have the same right?

good point

A Time to Speak Out

Inside Canada there are many things that we should take note of and speak out against. The symbols and traditions of our country are being eroded. The Monarchy is being undermined. A republic is being planned for by deliberate action. The parliamentary system is being reduced to a shadowy caricature. Cabinet Ministers come to Parliament at their will. The Prime Minister's office has become a place where multitudes of individuals sitting at desks do the thinking for the nation.

Ministers' speeches are so highly regarded that in a recent case they were being delivered by Brinks' vans. Normally one of the things that Brinks pride themselves on is that they carry bullion with security. Not even the most partisan dare conclude that Ministers' speeches are bullion!

The Trudeau Government is intent on bringing about the twilight of Parliament by the suppression of dissent in Parliament and outside. It has been boasted that the congressional system of government is to be brought into effect, apparently in imitation of the United States and the Republic of France. Parliament now is developing the shortcomings of both, and few of the virtues of either.

The changing of the rules not long ago is contributing to this change. The sending of legislation to committees has killed debate in Parliament. Few if any material changes occur in committee because, as the Member for East York said, instructions were given that Liberal Members must carry out the wishes of the Government. The change in the rules came in December 1968, when finally the Opposition agreed that if the Government would give up one rule (16(a)) the rest of the changes would be accepted. The Prime Minister two days later boasted that the Opposition had fallen into a trap that he had set for them. In 1969 Parliament was throttled by closure with an amend-

30

ment that has made the House of Commons a shadow.

Changes are taking place that are unknown to most Canadians. The Prime Minister, Gérard Pelletier, and Jean Marchand—the triumvirate —are using the Liberal party for their purposes, which have been made clear and definite and which are leading to a virtual socialization of Canada.

The Prime Minister said recently that a new Canada is being brought about under the present Government. He did not mention the "just society", for recently he said that it had become a slogan and he did not want to hear the expression any more. It is now a dirty word in his vocabulary.

Canadians find it hard to believe that freedom is being challenged. The Trudeau Government clearly does not believe in freedom. That was revealed when counsel for the Department of Justice on the Bill of Rights case before the Supreme Court of Canada argued strongly and powerfully against the Bill of Rights being interpreted as an instrument to preserve the freedom of Canadians.

Law-making has been turned over to a group of self-styled intellectuals who from their ivory towers, cut off from the rest of Canada, and receiving up to $30,000 or $32,000 a year, decide what shall be done. Then, with a servile Liberal membership, measures are pushed through the House of Commons and, while there is some desultory criticism in the Senate, the legislation presented is passed and becomes law.

Never has there been in Canada's peacetime history legislation brought in of so authoritarian a nature, the purpose being to increasingly centralize administration. An example of this was an Act to establish a National Farm Products Marketing Council which will make farmers across Canada the pawns of bureaucrats. The Government that does nothing effective for Canadians who are poor, for the veterans, and for the old-age pensioner, pours tens of millions of dollars into countries in French Africa.

The Trudeau Government seems to be dedicated to controlling the thinking of Canadians. Through the power being exerted by Pierre Juneau, as Chairman of the Canadian Radio and Television Commission, private radio and T.V. station proprietors in Canada are frightened to speak, fearful of being subject to the cancellation of their licences. One such station was CKPM in Ottawa, which dared to have an open line program critical of the Government. Pierre Juneau did come before a Committee of the House and he uttered lachrymose words in reply to the criticism levied at him that he wishes to determine what Canadians shall hear, and to deny them the right to listen to what they will. His attitude was different when he spoke to the Association of Private Broadcasting Companies and in effect stated: "When I ope my lips, let no dog bark." Under him the broadcasting network owned by the people of Canada is allowed to broadcast what he permits.

Past experience with Information Canada, under an arch-partisan, Jean-Louis Gagnon, whose past record indicated a leftist philosophy, demonstrated that the people of Canada were to have a political screening of public information.

What is being done by the Trudeau Government could be summed up in the words of Sukarno as "guided democracy" in which freedom of the individual is diminished and the power of the governing authority is multiplied.

3

The True Function of Parliament

"Parliament is a place honoured by tradition, and hallowed by the greatness of its history. Parliament is the place where your freedom and mine is preserved."

Parliament is the most maligned of our institutions. In every generation, during the three hundred years in which modern Parliament has existed, it has been the subject of criticism. In the last few years our institutions such as Parliament and the Monarchy are plainly being eroded. Some critics there are who advocate change out of a desire to improve; others wish to annihilate traditional institutions and symbols. Parliament has been a favourite subject of satirists and of columnists over the years. One hears questions such as "Why doesn't Parliament get down to work?", "Why does it talk so much?", "Why is there an Opposition?", "Why shouldn't Members go to Parliament and all unite?".

It should be understood that Parliament can deal only with legislative matters that the Cabinet decides to bring before it, excepting for the very limited right of the private Member to introduce bills other than money bills. The Cabinet places before Parliament its measures, and in discussion changes and improvements can be brought about.

Professor Ivor Jennings, the great English authority on Parliament said—and rightly— that "the function of Parliament is not to govern but to criticize, to modify Government

policy, and to educate public opinion". To
those who say that Parliament should be turning out legislation in quantity, my answer is
that its mission is freedom and the assurance
that all the people shall receive justice. It is not
a slot machine into which one drops a slug to
see the legislation come out.

Parliament is a place honoured by tradition
and hallowed by the greatness of its history.
Parliament is the place where your freedom
and mine is maintained and preserved. Freedom of speech is of the essence, but the exercise of that freedom is circumscribed by decent
behaviour and a respect for the rights of others.
By tradition, visitors were not allowed within
the confines of Parliament. No one is recognized as being in the gallery, even though a portion of the gallery has been set aside for the
press. At any time a Member may rise in his
place and say, "Mr. Speaker, I spy strangers",
and the galleries are emptied. That course was
followed once or twice during the Second
World War. The tradition originated in the
days of Pym and Eliot and Hampton, when
Charles I used to place people in the gallery to
make threatening signs to discourage Members
who were exercising their freedom of speech.

Members of the government and the Opposition sit facing each other eighteen feet apart. In
past times this meant they were beyond the
reach of each other's swords.

The Queen and the Governor General cannot go into the gallery of the House of Commons.

Parliament's paramount responsibility is the preservation of freedom. Its authority is legislative, and with it is exercised executive and administrative control. Its major responsibility is to require that expenditures of the people's monies shall be kept under control and that taxation shall not be levied without its majority consent. Parliament is the place in which abuses and grievances are aired and the rights of individuals are preserved.

Personally I think that there would be a great improvement in the standard of debate if the press of our country would give from day to day a short summary of what individual backbenchers have said. There is nothing more distressing for a young man coming into Parliament than to have no passing mention in the press, on radio, or T.V. *The Times* of London, while Parliament sits, gives each Member who participates in debates a couple of lines in the parliamentary report on the following day. The backbencher deserves more consideration than he is receiving. I realize that newspaper space is at a premium, but if this were done it would vastly improve the debate in Parliament and do away with the reading of speeches.

There has been some discussion regarding televising House of Commons debates. I have supported the idea and brought about the first televising of the Opening of Parliament in the 1957 fall session when Her Majesty the Queen opened Parliament.

If television is not brought into the House of Commons the prestige and importance of Parliament Hill will be further diminished because of the competition of a new forum that has been established in the foyer outside the main door of the House of Commons. Ministers of the Crown and other Members give their news to T.V. and radio. Ministers have given revised versions of the answers that they have just previously given in the House. On occasion, Ministers have furnished information that they denied to the House of Commons only a few minutes earlier.

Television should be brought into the House of Commons, so that the people of Canada can learn about Parliament, and become aware of issues, not through the revising eyes of news analysts or commentators but through their own eyes and ears. It may be well to start with the Question Period, but important debates should not be ignored. It may be that eventually a national television channel, perhaps a UHF channel using the satellite, will be covering Parliament daily. Until that comes about, the CBC and CTV could and should make available for fifteen minutes to one-half hour a day, either live or taped, the important oc-

currences or events or news of the House and
transmit them without editing and without
comment.

There is widespread failure to understand
the institution of Parliament. The very conti-
nuity and stability of the system of British
parliamentary democracy and the absence of
any constitutional upheavals may have induc-
ed a measure of contempt, bred of familiarity.
"The characteristic danger of great nations,"
said Walter Bagehot, "like the Roman or the
English, which have a long history of con-
tinuous creation, is that they may at last fail
from not comprehending the great institutions
which they have created."

The fact is that most Canadians take only a
superficial interest in the working of their
government. Some are indifferent, others con-
temptuous. In his *Essentials of Parliamentary
Democracy*, Professor R. Bassett wrote: "It is
this inadequate comprehension of the working
of our political system which is responsible for
excessive demands upon it, and for the resulting
disillusionment."

Lack of understanding, from whatever cause
it may arise, has created a mood of cynicism
and skepticism that could pose, if unanswered,
a grave danger to Canadian parliamentary
democracy.

I do not say that Parliament is perfect or that
there must not be change to meet changing con-

ditions, but changes should be based on experience rather than idealistic experiment.

Recent changes in the Rules of the House of Commons, now in effect, reveal the dangers of experiment.

The new rules came into force in the House of Commons in January, 1969. When introduced in the House, it was said the changes would give more power to committees of Parliament, and give private members greater opportunities. Committees were to be composed of all parties in proportions approximately equal to those of party membership in the Commons. It was argued that extension of the Committee System would enhance the importance of Members of Parliament and give them every opportunity to express their views effectively. The view was advanced that the complexity of legislation has made it impossible to ensure proper and careful study, clause by clause, of bills in the House of Commons. Such study was to take place in committees, whereby bills would be made more effective by amendments made in committee. It was contended that all legislation would be more meaningful and would reflect the considered opinions of the committee members.

The Government gave assurances that every opportunity would be given for members to express their views and, if acceptable to the majority of the committee, they would be translated into recommendations for amendment in the Report of the committee to the House.

I predicted that the Government would enforce its will over its supporters in the committees; that committees would be effective only on non-controversial matters, but that on controversial bills committee members would vote on a party basis.

It was pointed out that the committee system works in the Congress of the United States. It does work, and for good reason. Under the American system of government the executive and legislative bodies are separate and, as a consequence, changes by committee of legislation proposed by the president would in no way weaken the prestige or authority of the political party to which the president belongs. Under the British parliamentary system which Canada has adopted and adapted to its particular needs, defeat of a measure in committee, or substantial amendment would weaken, even destroy, the prestige of the government.

Several weeks went by and it was revealed how this new committee system would operate and how the freedom of expression of government members would be maintained. The Member for East York, a Government supporter, sent a circular letter to his constituents which revealed that the Whip of party discipline applied to committee members, and instructions were given that members of committees supporting the government must vote as the government determines regardless of their personal views. That revelation debunked the whole concept of the new committee plan.

Parliament is losing its image and becoming more and more, under the roster system, a nuisance to the Cabinet. It is true that in the United Kingdom, ministers appear to answer questions only on certain specified days. That is so, but the question period is radically different from that employed in Canada. At Westminster, questions are submitted in written form on the Order Paper, and a minister must appear (unless absent for sufficient reason) to answer them when any question applicable to his department is called. In Canada there is a daily confrontation for forty minutes of oral questions and, unless ministers make themselves available to answer questions, matters of urgency cannot be inquired into.

To summarize, it is my opinion that the heralded Committee System has not been effective and will not be effective. It has to a large extent removed from the House of Commons the examination of legislation and expenditures and has placed it in the hands of committees, which are powerless to act because of the shackles of party discipline. The net result has been that instead of the new committee system providing more freedom for

Members in the expression of their views, it has actually had the reverse result.

The argument is made that Parliament, under the new rules, is turning out more legislation than it used to produce. This is arguable, but Parliament has to be measured by the quality, not the quantity, of the laws that it turns out.

If the new rules had been in effect in 1911, it is within the realm of possibility that Canada might have become part of the United States. In that year Sir Wilfrid Laurier attempted to arrange a Reciprocity Agreement which would have had the effect of creating a partial customs union between Canada and the United States. American statesmen in favour of the Reciprocity measure exulted that with Reciprocity in effect, the independence of Canada would end. Sir Wilfrid Laurier brought the Reciprocity Bill to the House of Commons. The Opposition stood for months on that question of principle, and despite Laurier's substantial parliamentary majority, he was forced to go to the country on the issue when he could not get approval from the House, and he was defeated.

That would be impossible now. Time would be allocated, the Bill would be passed, and irreparable damage could be done. It is of interest that Laurier did not criticize the Opposition for obstruction or filibustering, and indeed he approved of a strong Opposition fighting day by day against his government.

Why is there an Opposition recognized under law and known as Her Majesty's Loyal Opposition? The Opposition is an essential part of parliamentary democracy. The nineteenth-century dictum of Lord Acton that: "Power tends to corrupt, and absolute power corrupts absolutely", remains as true today as when it was laid down. There is no protection for liberty simply in the word "democracy". Unchecked, the best of rulers become autocratic. It is the nature of man. Autocracy, tyranny, dictatorship, are shadows that ever stand in the wings of even the freest of parliaments. In the absence of a strong Opposition, a cabinet with a commanding position in the House could and would rule without regard to individual and minority rights.

"The democratic method", said Lord Hailsham (now the Rt. Hon. Quintin Hogg, M.P.), "is not that of securing formal agreement by enforcing acceptance of a minority or majority decree through the suppression of all opposition. On the contrary differences are recognized, and their adequate expression welcomed as a means of attaining voluntary and genuine accord. Countries cannot be fully free until they have an organized Opposition. It is not a long step from the absence of an organized Opposition to complete dictatorship."

45

Support for a similar view on political systems rather paradoxically comes from an apologist for the German Nazi revolution, Herr Friedrich Seiburg, who has written: "The Opposition is no less important than the ruling party, and this legitimization of the Opposition infuses an element of humanity into parliamentary government."

The need of a strong Opposition is supported by almost every political writer. Among these is Professor Bassett, who has stated that: "The Opposition is not merely tolerated, but treated as indispensable". He emphasizes the existence of an Opposition as an example of the difference between democracy and autocracy.

Opposition is as necessary to the parliamentary system as is the Cabinet. The two are inseparable. One without the other would mean tyranny or chaos. It is commonplace for all governments to view effective opposition as obstruction and this is a view too often and too lightly taken up by critics outside Parliament. An Opposition that discharges its parliamentary responsibilities properly is bound to appear to those opposed as obstructionist.

The weapon of the Opposition is discussion and argument. If the Opposition stand is not justifiable in the opinion of the people, the people are not slow to show their displeasure.

I have referred to the example of the great debate on Sir Wilfrid Laurier's Reciprocity Bill

in 1911. Another example was the 1912 Naval
Aid Bill introduced by the Government of Sir
Robert Borden with the aim of contributing
ships to the British Navy. The Liberal Opposition fought it for weeks and aroused public opinion to such an extent that, while it passed the
House of Commons under pressure, when it
came before the Senate it was turned down.
The Opposition discharged its function, and in
the light of subsequent constitutional development, the view the Opposition took was the
right one.

It is of the very essence of our system that,
when the Opposition feels strongly on a matter
of principle, and on matters of major and far-
ranging public concern, they must carry opposition to the utmost limit allowed by parliamentary usage.

Only a strong and alert Opposition can
check and control the excessive and unconstitu-
tional powers assumed by or conferred upon
bureaucrats, and to prevent short-cuts through
democratic procedure that Cabinets and
bureaucrats find so attractive and easy to take.

Without an Opposition functioning as a
recognized part of parliamentary proceedings,
government would degenerate into arbitrary
direction of public affairs by the executive and
the bureaucracy—minorities would stand unprotected—freedom would wither—individual
liberty would be in jeopardy—unwarranted and

oppressive invasion of private rights would grow unchecked.

Without an Opposition, the administration of the day could and would carry on the task of running the country, but such a situation would be identical with a totalitarian one-party state. Efficiency of administration was claimed by Hitler and Mussolini, but freedom died.

The House of Commons is, I fear, becoming less and less important and more impotent as the Prime Minister and Cabinet Ministers increase their control. Debate is becoming increasingly more pointless and ineffectual. There is little wonder that an increasing number of Members feel it is purposeless to make speeches. Yet I know from experience how beneficial critical debate can be. When I was Prime Minister, Government legislation was introduced which was felt to be well prepared and could not be challenged, but which had to be altered after well-argued criticism by one or two Members of the Opposition. Debate must be restored or Parliament will decline in the discharge of its mission of freedom.

The truth of the situation may be further illustrated by a short historical review of the growth and development of the office of the prime minister. Sir Robert Walpole more than two centuries ago was the first authentic Prime Minister in the modern sense. Up to his time the Sovereign had regarded the ministers of the cabinet as his personal representatives. The practice of the Sovereign's being present at the cabinet meetings ended in the reign of George I who, not understanding English, regarded his presence in the cabinet as unfruitful and unnecessary.

However, it was not until the middle of the eighteenth century that the expression "Prime Minister" came into use. It is worthy of note that the office of prime minister is not mentioned in the British North America Act, which embodies Canada's written constitution.

To achieve the prime ministership in the United Kingdom, the person so chosen must have been in the House of Commons for fifteen years on an average and have passed through the fires of political controversy. It is often said that a young man could be prime minister in these days. Legally he could but it would be difficult for him because he would lack the experience in the atmosphere of the House of Commons.

A prime minister's private life must be an open book. Privacy ends when he accepts the seals of office. It has been said that "the political star performer leads the actor's life", and is liable to the discipline of the clergy. With the franchise being made universal, the elections since have been largely personality contests between leaders, with two alternative prime ministers before the public. Politics have become personalized.

Political leaders depend on the information media. This was best expressed by Lord Esher in referring to Lloyd George: "He lived by the press and by the press he shall die."

The powers of the prime minister include control of the agenda for all cabinet sessions. Generally speaking nothing can be dealt with in the cabinet unless the prime minister so decides.

The following powers are the special prerogatives of the Prime Minister:

1. Appointment of:
   Privy Councillors
   Cabinet Ministers
   Lieutenant-Governors (including leave of
     absence to same)
   Provincial Administrators
   Speaker of the Senate
   Chief Justices of all Courts
   Senators
   Sub-Committees of Council
   Treasury Board
   Committee of Internal Economy, House of
     Commons
   Deputy Heads of Departments
   Librarians of Parliament
   Crown Appointments in both Houses of
     Parliament
   Governor General's Secretary's staff

2. Recommendations in any department.

The prime minister used to be regarded as a first among equals in the cabinet but since the First World War there are no equals. His powers are now so wide and general, there seems little question that a prime minister to-day in the British parliamentary tradition has greater power than the president of the United States.

4

Towards
a False
Republic*

"Those who advocate a republic,
knowing that it is impossible to obtain
their objective constitutionally, . . .
have apparently determined to do
indirectly and surreptitiously by
administrative action, what they
realize they cannot do directly."

*A speech delivered to the Empire Club of Toronto
on March 9, 1972.

Where is Canada going? I am appalled by what is taking place in my country. I speak as I feel personally, and my views may not be shared, but I am at an age when I must speak out, for it cannot be too long that I shall be able to do so.

In your heart of hearts have you not been asking yourself the question: "Where are we going?" What of our institutions? What is happening to Parliament to-day? It still consists of the Crown, the Senate and the House of Commons, but what of our Constitution?

The prestige of Parliament is being deliberately debased by rule changes until the private Members on the Government side are becoming cyphers or puppets of the Cabinet. Always through history those who want to bring about changes that ought not to be made plead for efficiency—efficiency, however, is not the measure of Parliament, however desirable; Parliament has a soul. It is not, as some theorists would have it be, a corporation in which the Prime Minister is the managing director, holding proxies over the majority of the stock, and dominating the rest of the shareholders. The Members have a right to their views, and ought not to be required to check their consciences at the door of the House of Commons as they come in because

the Government wants to bring about changes
that emasculate the Constitution.

Thirty-two years ago I came into the House
of Commons, and even though we were in the
darkest days of war Members by their speeches
brought about changes. No one was then a
"bigot" because he disagreed with the Government. The debates were living and vital, but no
one used opprobrious words and gestures about
political opponents that should require the use
of a strong detergent as mouthwash.

J. S. Woodsworth was totally opposed to
war, but was listened to with respect as he defended his views. The Hon. J. P. A. Cardin opposed conscription, but was listened to with
respect. Both were sincere, and sincerity is the
first qualification for an effective Member of
Parliament.

My views on the forced Japanese evacuation
from British Columbia during the war years
were in strong opposition to what was done,
and were not shared by more than a dozen
Members in the House, yet the House listened
and applauded. Members stayed in the House
because debates were interesting. Ministers
were present daily to answer questions, and
they did not follow the system of appearing
from time to time, like cuckoos in cuckoo
clocks.

There is a vocal minority today who demand
an end of the Monarchy. Indeed, it is ad-

vocated by some who occupy high positions in Government, and who have sworn allegiance to Her Majesty.

What is best for Canada, a monarchy or a republic? If Canadians, either by constitutional amendment or by their votes, decide in favour of a republic (and I do not believe they would), it would be accepted. But that does not justify what is happening. Gradually the traditions of our country are being torn asunder. The Hon. Mr. Pelletier, who has custody of the Seal of Canada, summed up his viewpoint in these words on a CBC television program, *Encounter,* as reported on July 20, 1970:

> Our Government has been accused of suppressing the Canadian coat of arms, but it really doesn't matter. We could put Schenley's [the distillers] coat of arms on government buildings and no one would know the difference. These symbols do not mean a thing in the twentieth century.

At the time of Confederation, with each and every Father of Confederation giving support, Canada became a constitutional monarchy. Section 9 of the British North America Act provides: "The executive Government and authority of and over Canada is hereby declared to continue and be vested in the Queen."

To change this would require a change in the

Constitution and in practice would require the support of the Senate, the House of Commons and the unanimous support of the provincial legislatures.

Those who advocate a republic knowing that it is impossible to attain their objective constitutionally, which would require that not only Parliament but all the Provinces agree, have apparently determined to do indirectly and surreptitiously by administrative action, what they realize they cannot do directly.

An example of administrative erosion of the Constitution is in the publication entitled *Organization of the Government of Canada*, which has been in use for eleven years.

In the issue of 1969 the true and actual constitutional portion was set out therein as follows:

The Executive power in Canada is vested in the Queen by the British North America Act, 1867. It consists of statutory power, which is derived from that Act and from legislation of Parliament and prerogative power, which may be described as a residual authority of the Sovereign as Head of the State. The Governor General is the Queen's representative in Canada. The Governor in Council exercises executive functions on behalf of the Queen.

In the next issue, dated July 1970, the Queen was abolished in these words, which were substituted for the constitutional position:

> Executive power in Canada is exercised by the Cabinet and carried out in the name of the Governor General who acts formally on the advice of the Privy Council. Cabinet Ministers who make up the Government of the day are, therefore, all Privy Councillors and as such take collective responsibility for giving advice to the Governor General, advice which by convention he is bound to accept.

There has been a change in the description of the role of the Governor General in the *Canada Year Book*. A passage in the 1969 *Canada Year Book* stating that the "primary responsibility of the Governor General . . . is to provide the nation with a Cabinet or Ministry capable of conducting *Her Majesty's* Government with the support of the House of Commons", was changed in the 1970-71 *Canada Year Book* to read: "The primary responsibility of the Governor General . . . is to provide the nation with a Government capable of carrying on with the support of the House of Commons."

An "Information Canada" booklet entitled *How Canadians Govern Themselves* states on page 3 that " . . . we are no longer a Dominion." This statement is a direct contradiction of the British North America Act which gave the name "Dominion of Canada" to our country, and that was the name included in the Treaty of Versailles, the operative Statute of Westminster and the Canadian declaration of war in 1939.

I have raised my voice continually against what has been done in recent years to undercut the constitutional position of the Queen, but no defence, or indeed any reply, has been given by a Prime Minister or any Minister. There was no answer that could have been given except to admit my contention.

The Royal Mail is no more. The uniforms of our armed forces, because they bore similarity to British uniforms, have been changed. The words "The Royal Canadian Mounted Police" have been removed from vehicles and buildings and "Police" substituted.

As to the usefulness of the Monarchy, I will appropriate the views of Canadians who have held the position of Queen's Representative. The Rt. Hon. Vincent Massey, in February 1965, summed up his views after a lifetime of experience as follows:

> The Crown plays some part, large or small, in everybody's life. The rights of the Monarch are indestructible and provide the quality of give and take vital to the working of Government. Canada has

always been a Monarchy. First, under France, then under England, and now under our own Queen.

Some people see more in a president than in a sovereign. I must tell you that, for our country, I can see only less. I am convinced that history has given us a system which, in a multi-racial nation such as ours, is more wise and workable than that which any theorist could invent.

The Monarchy is essential to us. Without it as a bastion of Canadian nationality, Canadian purpose and Canadian independence, we could not, in my view, remain a sovereign State.

It is to the Crown we can look to encourage the spirit of nationhood and to warn against its neglect. It is a trust that we have been given.

The Right Honourable Georges Vanier understood the meaning of the Monarchy. In his Inaugural remarks of September 15, 1959, he said:

The recent visit of our Sovereign to this country with His Royal Highness the Duke of Edinburgh, has made of the word loyalty a synonym of affection.

We are indeed fortunate in being attached to the Crown which holds for the world a promise of peace. It is well to recall that the Queen is the symbol of the free association of member nations of the Commonwealth and as such is accepted as its Head. The total area of the Commonwealth is estimated to be about fourteen and a half million square miles and its population something in the neighbourhood of six hundred and fifty millions.

It is of interest that the 1972 Speech from the Throne made provision for the introduction of legislation making "O Canada" our National Anthem, but there is no reference whatever to the Royal Anthem, "God Save The Queen". This in face of the recommendation of a committee of both Senate and Commons for joint action on both anthems.

What of the Constitution? It is being undermined and emasculated by the Languages Bill. I shall not be deterred by the fear of being designated a bigot. I am one who has stood for the constitutional rights of French Canadians long before becoming a Member of Parliament, and indeed, fifty years ago I was successful in winning on behalf of French-Canadian trustees a case concerning the use of the French language in the schools. I have always stood firmly for the constitutional rights of French Canada. It was under my administration that for the first time French became equal with English in the House of Commons by means of simultaneous translation. It was my recommendation that brought about the nomination by Her Majesty the Queen of Georges Vanier as Her Majesty's representative. Realizing that there was not a fair share of French Canadians in the higher brackets of the Civil Service and in the Foreign Service, I changed that.

I voted against the Languages Bill, and was one of seventeen M.P.s to do so. I voted contrary to my party's view because I believed that what was being done was to amend the Constitution by statute. I asked the Government to submit the questions to the Supreme Court of Canada as to whether or not what was being done was constitutional and whether the proposed statutory amendment was or was not a constitutional amendment. The Government refused, contending that it had no doubt that the proposed legislation was legal, and that what was being done was not a constitutional amendment. It was stated by the Minister of Justice that any Canadian could challenge its constitutionality. I contended that such a view was an untenable one.

The Hon. Joseph Thorson, former Minister in the Mackenzie King Government and subsequently President of the Exchequer Court of Canada, launched proceedings contending that what had been done was unlawful. The federal government, apparently fearing the result, successfully contended otherwise.

I belong to a minority who took the stand in June 1971, and still do, that Premier Bourassa was justified in preventing the implementation of the Victoria Charter, but for reasons other than he advanced.

I think that mature consideration has revealed many weaknesses in the Charter. With a large portion of the Charter there could be no disagreement, but there were several important sections which, in my opinion, would have frozen the Constitution irrevocably.

These may be summed up as follows: (1) the Bill of Rights would have been reduced to virtual innocuity; (2) it was claimed that the Supreme Court of Canada would be strengthened by appointments to that Court being subject to provincial consideration. In my view this change was based on a proposition that is a denial of the Rule of Law; that the judges appointed from the several provinces should have the approval of those provinces; (3) the formula for future amendments to the Constitution would deny the provinces of Saskatchewan and Manitoba any rights concerning amendments, as a result of the weighting against them in the proposed amending formula. These provinces would have been forced to accept amendments whether their citizens accepted them or not.

As proposed, amendments to the Constitution could be made in future by resolutions passed by a majority vote in the Parliament of

Canada, along with majorities in those provinces which have 25 per cent of the population of the nation (such provinces being Ontario and Quebec), along with two of the four Atlantic provinces and two of the four Western provinces. However, this would deny any effective say to the provinces in the West which have less than 50 per cent of the total population of the four provinces in that grouping. It is inconceivable that for many years to come, if ever, the provinces of Manitoba and Saskatchewan would in population equal 50 per cent of the total population of the four provinces. The result is that they would be second-class provinces within the nation; (4) the protection which education in the English language has in the Province of Quebec under the B.N.A. Act would have been removed.

The pursuit of constitutional amendment and patriation of our Constitution must not be given up. I still feel that the proposal advanced by me in February 1963 should be tried, as all other courses have failed. Invitations for a National Constitutional Conference were to be sent to the provinces. What I had in mind was that the representatives would not sit for one, two, or three days, but would sit indefinitely, as was the case of the Conferences in Quebec and Charlottetown prior to Confederation. The Conference would be charged with agreements to patriate the Constitution and to make such amendments in the B.N.A. Act as would correct injustices that exist and which, uncorrected, would lead to misunderstanding and even disunity. The task would have been a monumental one, to preserve the principles of Confederation and to round out and restate Canada's goals.

With the advent of the Pearson Government this Conference came to nought. In my opinion it should be convened now, but with the membership including not only federal and provincial government representatives, but also representatives of the Opposition parties in the federal government and each of the provinces; and in addition representatives of national organizations such as the Royal Canadian Legion, the Empire Club, the St. Jean Baptiste Society, and the various ethnic groups, to the end that all Canadians will be involved in remaking the Constitution.

To bring about One Canada—One Nation would be its watchword. There should be no special status but equal status for all provinces. There should be the acknowledgment of a basic condition of Confederation, which, although not expressly stated in the B.N.A. Act, was accepted by all the Fathers—that no province once having joined Confederation could secede of its own volition.

Virulent Anti-Americanism

In the international area I shall refer only
to Canada-U. S. A. relations. A hurricane of
virulent anti-Americanism is in full sway. It is
dangerous. The United States is understandably
annoyed with our country about some of the
statements that were made in Moscow by
Canada's leader some months ago, that Canadians fear the United States economically (and
I can understand that), and culturally (I can
understand that from some viewpoints), but
when, inexcusably, "even militarily" was added,
it led to feelings of annoyance, antagonism, and
even rage as to whither Canada is going.

We must welcome American investment in
Canada. During my period of office I was
called anti-American for saying that Canada
should make clear that Canadian subsidiaries
of American companies must observe Canadian
law and should make their policies with
Canada and no other nation, however friendly,
in mind.

As Prime Minister I was criticized because I
dared to take the stand that Canada's policies
would be made in Canada by Canadians. That
view was accepted by President Eisenhower,
but was regarded by President Kennedy as
heresy, and indeed, he did everything he could
to defeat my Government, and succeeded in

doing so in 1963. My offence was that I dared to believe that Canada should make its own policies while co-operating fully with the United States on behalf of freedom.

I am not unmindful of the fact that after his visit to Washington some months ago, the Prime Minister was rendered enthusiastic if not ecstatic by the words of the President of the United States, that Canada was not regarded as a colony of the United States, nor does Washington regard Canada's economy as being under the domination of the United States.

The President could not speak for the international power corporations. Indeed, the view of many of them was expressed by the president of the U. S. National Coal Association when giving evidence in the U. S. Senate in May 1971. He stated: "Our Government considers Canada our own for energy purposes".

President Nixon, in June 1971, stated that there was a crisis in the U. S. resources and that resolving it would require vast quantities of energy from Canada. Some Americans argue that Canada's future needs should not be considered. This is something that Canada, if it is to survive, cannot agree to. Faced with increasing economic competition from Japan and the European Common Market, and having depleted itself of many of its own raw materials, it is natural for the United States to turn towards

Canada's resources. Such a concept as the creation in Canada of a free U. S. market in energy and raw material resources would destroy this nation.

How significant Canadian resources are is revealed by a recent estimate by Dr. Preston Cloud, professor of bio-geology of the University of California, that the world will run out of natural gas, zinc, tin, gold, silver and platinum in twenty years. He said:

> In thirty years there will be no uranium 235, the basic atomic fuel. In about fifty years, oil will have ceased to gush from the last well. In less than a century we will have used up all our supplies of nickel, tungsten and copper. And many other minerals are in similar danger. Only iron has a life expectancy of 400 years.

Action must be taken to protect Canadian sovereignty but I do not accept the high hopes of the Canada Development Corporation in purchasing back American investment or of the taking over by public enterprise of these resources. I am absolutely opposed to a screening commission for foreign investment. Such a commission could not but lead to political, even partisan considerations having precedence over economic reality.

The recent announcement that the Ontario Government will pay a larger share of school operating costs this year is worthy of commendation. The Province will raise its share of total operating costs from 60 per cent to 63 per cent. Taxes on real property are driving Canadians out of their homes and into apartments. In my opinion the taxation of domestic property, which bears too much of the costs of primary and secondary education, is as out of date in this jet age as is the Model T Ford.

The School Board revenues raised by local taxation in 1968 amounted to $1,434.5 millions. In 1969 to $1,584 millions, and the estimate for 1970, $1,774 millions, was the latest available figure. Too much rests on the local property tax as the main source of financing for primary and secondary education. President Nixon recently stated in a speech to Congress that:

Soaring school costs and soaring property tax rates threaten both our communities and our schools. They threaten communities because property taxes—which more than doubled in the ten years from 1960 to 1970—have become one of the most oppressive and discriminatory of all taxes, hitting most cruelly at the elderly and the retired; and they threaten schools, as hard-pressed voters understandably reject new bond issues at the polls.

The President said that he intends to relieve

the burden of property taxation and to provide for fair and adequate financing. I use his words when he said:

> The secret of mastering change in today's world is to reach back to old and proven principles, and to adapt them, with imagination and intelligence, to the new realities of a new age.

As a result of the Technical and Vocational Training Act the federal government contributes up to 75 per cent of the costs to assist in the financing of technical education. While education is exclusively a provincial responsibility, this arrangement was made without infringement on the jurisdiction of the provinces in the field of education.

I think the time has come to consider the bringing in of similar or analogous legislation for secondary education. The federal government can and should contribute towards the cost of providing educational facilities for all Canadians. A plan can be worked out which would give a firm guarantee (such as was given when the Technical and Vocational Training Act was brought about) that will assure financial assistance would not in any way constitute intrusion into the province's exclusive rights in the field of education. Since all Canadians should be equal in their citizenship rights, surely it is not too much to expect that the provincial departments of education would aim to make their various curricula relatively uniform. I have in mind that the financing should be done on the basis of a formula whereby the provincial departments of education would estimate the per pupil per day cost of the school board's areas or districts within their respective provinces. To do so would take into account salaries of teachers and other expenditures including carrying charges, etc. The total amount of such expenses when ascertained would be amortized over a period of at least thirty years. The federal government would pay to the provinces a share of the total costs, which I would consider should be between 40 per cent and 60 per cent. Such a plan, when carried into effect, would pay tremendous dividends in citizenship in making for better educated Canadians. There will be objections to it raised, as there were before the enactment of the Technical and Vocational Training Act which has made possible the technical training of several hundred thousands of Canadians who otherwise would not have received that training. This legislation has been set aside, as has the Productivity Council which my Government set up. Objections had been raised by constitutional authorities that the plan would impinge upon the exclusive jurisdiction of the provinces. We consulted with the provinces and arrived at agreement with all the provinces.

The load of taxation on homes, which furnishes so much toward the cost of elementary and secondary education, must be reduced.

What of the future? My view is that the federal government must take over a considerable share of the cost of education without at the same time interfering in any way with the exclusive jurisdiction of the provinces.

5

Pro-Canadians and Anti-Americans*

"Canadians strive for the preservation of their distinctive characteristics and above all for the right to determine Canada's destiny in Canada and by Canadians. ... It is not anti-American for Canadians to be concerned over their interests."

*Address delivered at Purdue University, Lafayette, Indiana, March 4, 1970.

I regard your invitation to speak at this University as a great honour and—your president was kind enough to suggest that we should speak of those things that Canada shares with the United States as well as those things that erect differences between us—a special opportunity to examine once again the field of Canadian-American relations.

A mark of this great college is that it strives for truth as it was defined by Sir William Osler, the world-famous Canadian medical doctor, in these words: "The truth is the best that you can get with your best endeavour—the best that best men accept."

Mahatma Gandhi defined the harvest of truth in these words: "Truth is like a vast tree—it yields more and more fruit the more you nurture it."

Good relations between our nations are like unto Gandhi's great tree, which yields more and more fruit the more it is nurtured and cared for.

The United States carries a tremendous responsibility, which was described by the Right Honourable Sir Winston Churchill in the Fulton speech of March 5th, 1946: "The United States stands at this time at the pinnacle of world power. It is a solemn moment for the

American democracy. For with primacy in power is also joined an awe-inspiring accountability to the future."

New to power, steeped in liberty, a stranger to tyranny, the United States has had to take over the world leadership which Great Britain willingly discharged for many generations. But now, having laid her all on the altar of freedom, Britain may be described by these words of Matthew Arnold: "A weary Titan . . . staggering on to her goal, bearing on shoulders immense, Atlantean, the load, well nigh not to be borne, of the too vast orb of her fate."

Canadians and Americans need constantly to engage in a dialogue of understanding. Their relationship demands frankness, candour, and forthrightness. Our nations have a long record of amity, co-operation and peace, beginning in 1794 by the Treaty of Amity, Commerce and Navigation which undertook "to promote a disposition favourable to friendship and goodwill".

The Rush-Bagot Agreement of 1817 provided for limits to the size of armed naval forces on the Great Lakes. It must have seemed unbelievable at the time of the Agreement that the events of war, so fresh in memory, could ever be forgotten; the destruction of the public buildings of the City of Toronto, the burning of the White House in Washington, and the threats of a "war of extermination".

For more than a century and a half we have learned to trust one another. No hereditary animosities or ancestral fears divide us. In Canada, we know that if the United States had not assumed world leadership since the last war, the free world would not have survived.

The measure of warm friendship which has for long existed between the United States and Canada, and the parallel interests of the two countries enables us to speak to each other with a measure of forthrightness which is permitted to very few countries in the world. The candour with which we can communicate with each other strengthens our understanding of each other and helps us to avoid the pitfalls of misunderstanding which have bedevilled relations of so many other countries in the world.

I would make it very clear that Canadians strive for the preservation of their distinctive characteristics and above all for the right to determine Canada's destiny in Canada and by Canadians. Canadians can be different from Americans without having serious differences with Americans. There are some who say that this attitude is anti-American. It is not anti-American for Canadians to be concerned over their interests. It is pro-Canadian.

Differences in the realm of power between our countries lead to misunderstandings. Some there are who assume the weaker must always support the course of action chosen by the stronger. At another extreme, there are those whose automatic response in almost every situation is to disagree.

Geography has placed the United States in front of us and Russia behind us, or to use the words of an eminent Canadian publicist, "When a Canadian looks at the world he does so through, past, or over the United States. The people south of the Great Lakes and the 49th parallel get in the way of his vision." To appreciate what freedom means as practised by our two countries, one must realize what Canada's tragedy would be if the U.S.S.R. were in the same geographical position in relation to Canada as is the United States of America.

In my opinion neither nation can fulfil its destiny in isolation from the other and neither nation can make its full contribution to freedom except in partnership with the other. Embracing the greater part of the continent of North America is a powerful nation, strong economically, which in less than twenty-five years has assumed world responsibility, and adjacent to it a nation, one-tenth its population, but no less unselfish over the years in the defence of freedom.

The United States has taken over the international responsibilities which Great Britain carried for several hundred years and has poured out its blood and treasure for freedom as has no other nation in history.

Canada's contribution to freedom in this century is not so widely known. In two World Wars and in Korea Canada served. Canada entered both World Wars voluntarily—in August 1914 and in September 1939. Few realize that in the First World War, with a population of only 8½ million people, the number of Canadians killed in action was 56,625, which is a larger number than the mortal casualties suffered by the United States. In the Second World War, the number of Canada's dead, based on population, was proportionate to that of the United States—the total in two World Wars being over 100,000 in the armed services.

Constitutional Differences

Canada and the United States have followed different constitutional courses. My country achieved its freedom and independence by evolution, not revolution—by its adherence to a limited monarchy within the Empire and now the Commonwealth of Nations, rather than through the establishment of a republic. While the Commonwealth knows no written constitution or agreement, it is bound by the aspirations of peoples in all parts of the globe who, while independent, are united in their dedication to freedom under the intangible unity of the Crown. Canada pays no part of the Queen's indemnity or allowances.

Legislative freedom is enshrined in our country in a Cabinet chosen by the prime minister who, as leader of the majority party in an elected House of Commons, is called upon to accept office by the Crown. We are sovereign in our law-making as in everything else. Our criminal law is common to all provinces. Our judiciary is appointed for life, and every legislator in Canada is elected by the people, with the exception of the members of the Senate.

In spite of our constitutional differences, the United States and Canada have achieved freedom as joint heirs of British freedom. Our shrines are your shrines—Westminster Hall, Independence Hall, and Mount Vernon. Our parliamentary institutions and our common law, although applied by us in different ways, are a common heritage. Magna Charta and the Bill of Rights are our joint inheritance—the Declaration of Independence, the first Ten Amendments to the Constitution, have made us joint tenants. These are the golden threads in the tapestry of freedom. From these Canada and the United States have achieved what Lincoln said of the American Declaration of Independence, that it had made possible "liberty not alone for the people of this country but hope to all the world for all future time".

Vietnam

While there are vast international problems in which the United States is involved, the one that today has all but monopolized the thinking of mankind is the war in Vietnam. Everyone is giving advice to Washington, while the United States, with the assistance of Australia, New Zealand, and South Korea, pours out its blood and treasure.

While I do not think that President Kennedy should have put armed forces in Vietnam, there can be no withdrawal without a political settlement or victory once the die has been cast. I believe that had it not been for strong United States action in Vietnam, Southeast Asia would by now have been overrun. The Communist Chinese plan was to crush Southeast Asia by co-operation and joint action with the Communists of Indonesia.

If it had not been for the United States' initiative in Vietnam, the anti-Communists in Indonesia would never have been able to stand firm. The Communist coup in Indonesia in October 1965 might — even would — have succeeded but for the inspiration that came to the anti-Communists who knew that the United States would not desert them.

I believe that the neutralization of a large area of Southeast Asia (including North and South Vietnam, Cambodia, and Laos) and guaranteed by the United States, Great Britain, Russia, and France, is basic to any settlement; that the question of unification of North and South Vietnam should be left to the two countries to be decided by a democratic decision of the people of both countries; that the general principles declared by the Geneva Conference of 1954 would be the basis for a cease-fire, and that any agreement arrived at would require a Supervisory Control Force to assure the implementation of the terms when agreed to.

Canada would be prepared to make her contribution to a Supervisory Control Force in Vietnam. Canada is providing not only elements for the United Nations force, but paying for them as well—the only nation that is doing so.

While there are people in Canada who ad-

81

vocate that the United States should withdraw from Vietnam, to do so, in my opinion, would be an act of retreat and surrender to the powers of Communism and would mean the gallop of Communism across Southeast Asia.

The United States, under the leadership of your President, has done everything possible to bring about a just settlement not only at the conferences in Paris over Vietnam, but as well in unilaterally reducing the numbers of American armed forces. The President has shown not only a desire but a strong initiative for negotiation. Negotiation is not a one-sided street and the refusal of the North Vietnamese, bolstered by Communist China, to negotiate anything is too often lost sight of by those who criticize. The United States' plans to aid the South Vietnamese to increase their defence potential, including a mutual withdrawal of non-South Vietnamese forces from South Vietnam and international free elections, reveal a statesmanlike determination.

One factor that indicates to me the total ruthlessness of North Vietnam is its refusal to follow any humanitarian principle respecting the almost 1,500 United States servicemen who have been reported as missing. The North Vietnamese have banished from their thinking regard for every principle of humanity on prisoners of war under the provisions of the Geneva Convention of 1944.

Defence

It is a challenging and dangerous fact that in operational intercontinental missiles the United States' superiority five years ago was 710. Today it has fewer of these missiles than has the U.S.S.R. by 236. However, in submarine-launched ballistic missiles, the United States today has over two to one, having 656 to the Soviets' 300.

To those who believe that the danger of war is over, the President's words in his recent speech need to be underlined and emphasized over and over again:

First, the Soviets' present build-up of strategic forces, together with what we know about their development and test programs, raises serious questions about where they are headed and the potential threats we and our allies face. These questions must be faced soberly and realistically.

While hoping that the safeguard program of Anti-Ballistic Missile Defence would not have been necessary, the facts of life and survival itself demand that these defences are proceeded with in whole or in part.

I believe that the peace of the world cannot be achieved without peace in Europe and those who advocate the withdrawal from NATO, whether in Canada or the United States, do a disservice to peace. I personally do not give support to the reductions in the NATO forces that Canada has made in the last year or so.

I was glad to note that the President on February 18 [1970], in his Foreign Policy Review to Congress, in bringing about a new and co-operative partnership of Free Nations, reaffirmed the United States' commitment to partnership with Europe. I was particularly impressed with his view that for too long in the past the United States had led without listening, talked to our allies instead of with them, and informed them of new departures instead of deciding with them.

There is one field in connection with NATO that requires attention and this is the economic co-operation as provided for in Article 2 of the NATO Pact, which reads as follows: "to strengthening their free institutions . . . promoting conditions of stability and well-being and encouraging economic collaboration."

There are continuing disagreements among the nations of NATO about what forces and other resources should be provided to the common cause.

It is sometimes contended by a vociferous minority that Canada should withdraw from her defence commitments. I have no ear for the lullabies of the neutralist—neither have the overwhelming majority of Canadians. Indeed, until such time as an effective international disarmament agreement has been negotiated, the Western nations must continue to maintain their defences.

All mankind hopes for a thaw in the frigid isolation of the U.S.S.R.

The lexicon of Communist abuse against the West has not been exceeded by the inter-party campaign of strife between Communist China and the U.S.S.R.

This amelioration of East-West relations seems to be the result of Russia's growing concern over China, which makes better relations with the West more desirable to, and by, the U.S.S.R.

Although Soviet tactics are unpredictable, the changed attitude gives ground for new hope for better relations than have existed since the end of World War I.

The offer made by the U.S.S.R. was to have convened a conference of the Warsaw Pact Nations and the NATO Nations and to establish a Security Pact. The U.S.S.R. never does anything without having a plan. My belief is that the reason for the U.S.S.R.'s making the effort arises because of its fear of Communist China and the increasing danger to U.S.S.R. because of the production of nuclear weapons by Communist China.

It would be helpful to the Soviet if an agreement could be secured, for having done so the representatives of the Soviet Union could then bargain strongly with Communist China on the basis that if war comes between their two countries, the U.S.S.R. will be freed from any danger of a "second front" against the U.S.S.R. taking place in Western Europe.

When I was Prime Minister, Canada entered into an agreement with the United States in 1957 to establish NORAD, which provided for a joint control of the Air Defence Forces in North America of Canada and the United States. We entered into this agreement because we recognized the security of this continent demanded close defence co-operation between both countries.

We decided later, in view of the danger of Soviet bomber attacks, to have two of the 36 Bomarc bases armed with nuclear weapons located on Canadian soil. Within a year or two the danger of bomber attacks by the U.S.S.R. had been greatly, if not completely, diminished. The Government I had the honour to lead from 1957 to 1963 accepted this premise and decided that the Bomarc bases armed with nuclear warheads as a defence against Russian bombers were no longer needed, and while two had been established on Canadian soil—largely financed by the United States—that with the changed conditions we should not arm these bases with nuclear weapons. We concluded that to do so would constitute a first step in the proliferation of nuclear weapons and would encourage other nations to ask for the nuclear deterrent.

In the Report of the President to Congress on February 18 [1970], he said this:

> The last 25 years have seen a revolution in the nature of military power. In fact, there has been a series of transformations — from the atomic to the thermonuclear weapon, from the strategic bomber to the intercontinental ballistic missile, from the surface missile to the hardened silo and the missile-carrying submarine, from the single to the multiple warhead, and from air defence to missile defence. We are now entering an era in which the sophistication and destructiveness of weapons present more formidable and complex issues affecting our strategic posture.

No statement could more completely bear out the stand taken by the Government I had the honour to lead when it decided that, while the bomber was a danger when the Bomarc agreements were entered into, with the passing of time the Bomarc as a defence against bombers became no longer needed. Indeed, if we were to have accepted nuclear weapons we felt that we would be providing an excuse for other nations to secure nuclear and atomic weapons and with proliferation there would be a major danger to mankind. Today the stand we took is accepted by all western nations and by the United States when it ratified the Non-proliferation Treaty.

Interference in Canadian Affairs

In 1963 there was gross interference in the general election campaign and prior thereto in statements made and issued by the State Department in Washington, including a declaration by the Secretary of State against the Canadian Government's stand over our decision not to accept nuclear weapons for Bomarc missiles. There was financial and organizing assistance given to the Liberal Party by Washington during the general election campaign of 1963.

There were earlier examples of a similar attitude by the Kennedy administration. For example, when the Canadian Government decided to approve the sale of wheat to Communist China on credit terms, so strong was the opposition to Canada's policy that the Kennedy administration endeavoured to prevent a Canadian corporation whose parent company was in the United States from supplying Canada with the necessary loaders so that the wheat could be shipped to Communist China. Canada took the stand that while it would not sell strategic material to Communist countries, including Cuba, trade in non-strategic commodities should be encouraged. This was regarded as heresy in Washington in 1961. That such a viewpoint is no longer so regarded was made clear in President Nixon's Foreign Affairs Report to Congress when he said that "specific steps have been taken towards easing economic relations between the United States and Communist China".

Sale of Water to the United States

I have time to refer only briefly to one or two other areas of Canadian-American relations. There is pressure at present for consideration of possible supply of large amounts of water from Canada for American use. I believe that we should not make any agreement at this time, nor for several years until our foreseeable future demands for water are known. Water once bargained away will be lost to our economic industrial expansion which, as I foresee it, will be very substantial.

American Investment in Canada

Capital from the United States has played an important role in the development of Canadian resources. We welcome this investment and we provide the best foreign investment climate in the world.

Canadians ask that American companies investing in Canada should not regard Canada as an extension of the American market; that they should be incorporated as Canadian companies making available equity stock to Canadians. That there is cause for questioning seems clear when I tell you that it is estimated that of American-controlled firms operating in Canada, not more than one in four offers stock to Canadians.

90

Agriculture

Canada has a carry-over of wheat which amounts to 1,000 million bushels this year. Canada must be able to compete for her share of the markets of the world, and will, I trust, providing other nations follow recognized competitive practices.

Nations joined in freedom should not follow policies which economically weaken their partners in freedom. Without an International Wheat Agreement that is carried out by the signatories, there can be no stability for Canada.

I have pressed over the years, but unsuccessfully, for the establishment of a World Food Bank. I believe that those nations possessing food surpluses will be held responsible in the pages of history for starvation in so many parts of the world. In the establishment of a World Food Bank, two results would follow—there would be available food for distribution internationally, and the danger of collapsing world prices, by the overhanging surplus of wheat, would be removed.

Aid to Underprivileged Countries

The wealth of continental resources and skills make high living standards possible for Canadians and Americans. Our eyes and our hearts must always look out to the world where "the abyss of affluence" divides peoples, and where bridges must be built to cross that abyss if the "developed North" and the "underdeveloped South" on this planet are to reach out and make true contact with each other. The world cannot exist half rich and half poor, and it is to the interests of all who love freedom that a favourable balance in the massive imbalance of human welfare be attained without delay.

The total expenditure for Canadian aid programs since 1951 has amounted to $2,125,300,000.

The massive and unprecedented U.S. Foreign Aid Program reveals the tremendous scope of the United States' world-wide interests today, and is an indication of the extent to which world peace rests upon U.S. determination to place its treasure and its benevolent might at the service of mankind.

6

Equality
and the
Bill of Rights

"The Drybones judgment makes it clear that as long as the Bill of Rights is on the statute books, it is, in matters under federal jurisdiction, the protector of the liberties of every Canadian, however humble."

It is natural that law and politics should be associated. Each deals with relations between human beings. Law is a science—politics an art. I write as one who tried in his lifetime to encourage, preserve and maintain freedom. Indeed, it took me forty years of advocacy to bring about a Bill of Rights. Naturally I was greatly pleased with the major advance in the march of freedom which came about in the judgment of the Supreme Court of Canada in the Drybones case in 1970.

That judgment decides that the Bill of Rights does and will protect the rights of Canadians in the preservation of the fundamental freedoms.

Since the Bill of Rights became the law of Canada in 1960, it has been subjected to all kinds of criticism and disparagement by some law professors and some politicians. They contended that the Bill of Rights was but a pious declaration of freedom, and no more. The Drybones judgment makes it clear that as long as the Bill of Rights is on the statute books, it is in respect of matters under federal jurisdiction the protector of the liberties of every Canadian, however humble.

The Canadian Bill of Rights has become by this judgment of Canada's highest court a vital instrument to free the minds of Canadians from the dread cancer of discrimination.

The Bill of Rights has now become recognized as a law under which fundamental freedoms will be protected for all, including the poor, the dispossessed, the ignored and the shut-out. It is now a sword and buckler in freedom's never-ending war against the forces which would destroy it; rather than a decorative feather duster, as some critics said or hoped it would be.

When Prime Minister, I tried to bring about an amendment to the constitution to entrench the Bill of Rights. Prime Minister Trudeau has tried. Both of us have failed. In my opinion, it will be many, many years, if ever, before all the provinces will allow their exclusive jurisdiction over civil rights to be abrogated or diminished in any way by a constitutional Bill of Rights.

Freedom in the final analysis demands the maintenance of the Rule of Law. More and more the Rule of Law is becoming a diminishing concept. The old principle that "to be free is to live under a government by law" has little or no application to the vast body of administrative regulations which are too often above the law.

The history of the last fifty years reveals a constant conflict between individualism and increasing bureaucracy through which government increases its intrusion into fields that should be reserved for the individual. Parliaments pass laws, but because of the vast complexity of modern conditions boards and other delegated institutions become major lawmakers. Parliamentarians endeavour (consciously or not) to limit liberty only to the extent that the people as a whole are prepared to accept such limitation in the general interest of all the people.

The Drybones judgment of the Supreme Court of Canada, in 1970, has quickly been recognized in our courts as a landmark of legal interpretation. It is of interest to all Canadians concerned with civil liberties to review briefly the facts of this case and the arguments that prevailed in the highest court of the land.

The evening of April 8, 1967, was an evening like any other in April in the bar of the Old Stope Hotel at Yellowknife in the Northwest Territories of Canada. A waiter noticed an Indian had fallen asleep at one of the tables, and he ejected him from the bar. The time was 10:50 p.m. Within the hour, Mrs. Hilda Rasche, assistant to the manager of the hotel, called the Royal Canadian Mounted Police to complain that an Indian was in the lobby of the hotel in an intoxicated condition. Constables Wool and Pertson, who were on duty, investigated the complaint and placed the Indian under arrest. His name was Joseph Dry-bones.

The offence charged against Joseph Dry-bones is not one that is unfamiliar to the Canadian public. It is the most common of all offences that may lead an individual to make acquaintance with the workings of our courts. It is the offence of being drunk in a public place. As the Liquor Ordinance of the Northwest Territories puts it in language common to all the provinces: "19. (1) No persons shall . . . (a) be in an intoxicated condition in a public place; . . .". The penalty, in the Northwest Territories, as in most provinces, is a fine not exceeding $50 and/or imprisonment for not more than 30 days. But Parliament, in its wisdom before the days of racial equality in Canada, had provided more severe penalties for Indians convicted of being drunk in a public place. The Indian Act provided a minimum fine of $10, whereas there was no minimum for the intoxicated white man, and a potential prison term of three months rather than 30 days. So it was Section 94 of the Indian Act under which Joseph Drybones was charged and Section 94 says: "An Indian who . . . (b) is intoxicated . . . off a reserve, is guilty of an offence and is liable on summary conviction to a fine of not less than $10 and not more than $50 or to imprisonment for a term not exceeding three months or to both fine and imprisonment."

There you have an example of the most blatant discrimination. The Indian faced a fine of at least $10, while the white man might not be fined at all; the Indian might be imprisoned for three months, the white man for a maximum of 30 days. A precise example of the evil of discrimination in Canadian justice, this is the kind of thing that the Canadian Bill of Rights declared at an end and, as the precedent of the Joseph Drybones case shows, we may expect to be ended in the actual proceedings of the Canadian courts.

But to return to the arrest of Joseph Drybones in Yellowknife, that evening in April 1967—a time when many Canadians of all racial stocks were thinking about plans to celebrate the centenary of Canada—we find that a few complications had arisen. The question of identification arose when it was learned that the Yellowknife Dogrib Indian band had three members named Joseph Drybones!

Two days after his arrest, Joseph Drybones pleaded guilty and was convicted by Justice of the Peace, John Anderson-Thompson. The point about whether the offence occurred "off the reserve", as the Indian Act specifies, was disposed of by testimony from Daniel Konelsky, secretary-treasurer of the Town of Yellowknife, who said that the Old Stope Hotel was indeed within the boundaries of the Town of Yellowknife and that the municipal files did not disclose any Indian reserves within the said boundaries. Testimony was heard from Chief Joe Sangris of the Yellowknife Dogrib band, who confirmed that the arrested man was indeed Joseph Drybones, with whom he was well acquainted, and that he was the Joseph Drybones who was married to Madeline Crapeau. It was David Grey Eyes, the regional director of Indian affairs at Fort Smith, N.W.T., who contributed the fact that there were two other members of the Dogrib Indian band at Yellowknife by the name of Joseph Drybones.

Counsel for Joseph Drybones moved the case by way of appeal to the Territorial Court, where the judge who heard the case, Mr. Justice W. G. Morrow, permitted the accused man to change his plea from guilty to not guilty. On June 5, 1967, Mr. Justice Morrow dismissed the conviction because it was contrary to the Canadian Bill of Rights. The Crown prosecutor then appealed the dismissal to the Court of Appeal of the Northwest Territories, and it upheld the judgment of Mr. Justice Morrow. The Crown then appealed to the Supreme Court of Canada, which confirmed the finding that the Indian Act under which Joseph Drybones had been charged was inoperative by virtue of the Canadian Bill of Rights. The decision was split six to three.

The issue before the Supreme Court was whether the offence of intoxication, provided in the Indian Act with penalties of a fine and imprisonment, was superseded by the Canadian Bill of Rights. The familiar "30 days" penalty for drunkenness in Canadian law, for instance, becomes "three months" in the Indian Act. Similarly, the Indian Act provides a minimum fine of $10 for the offence of intoxication, whereas the liquor ordinance of the Northwest Territories, where many Indians reside, imposes no minimum fine.

The relevant sections of the Canadian Bill of Rights under which these provisions of the Indian Act were argued to be inoperative were:

1. It is hereby recognized and declared that in Canada there have existed and shall continue to exist without discrimination by reason of race, national origin, colour, religion or sex, the following human rights and fundamental freedoms, namely . . .

    (b) the right of the individual to equality before the law and the protection of the law . . .

2. Every law of Canada shall, unless it is expressly declared by an Act of the Parliament of Canada that it shall operate notwithstanding the Canadian Bill of Rights, be so construed and applied as not to abrogate, abridge or infringe or to authorize the abrogation, abridgment or infringement of any of the rights or freedoms herein recognized and declared . . .

The majority judgment in the Drybones case was written by Mr. Justice Ritchie. The five concurring justices were Fauteux, Martland, Judson, Spence, and Hall, with Mr. Justice Emmett Hall adding reasons of his own. The dissenting view was written by Mr. Justice Pigeon who was supported by Chief Justice Cartwright and Mr. Justice Abbott. It is of interest to present the reasons given by Mr. Justice Ritchie for the majority view and much of his text is found in the Appendix.

Mr. Justice Hall, in giving his reasons for concurring with the judgment that the Bill of Rights applied to Indians as well as to all other Canadian citizens, referred to an American precedent. The United States Supreme Court in 1953 reversed its own decision of 1896 which had supported the idea of the "separate but equal" standing of Negroes and others—a clear defence of segregation. Mr. Justice Hall noted that the 1896 judgment had upheld the "separate but equal" doctrine, that equality of treatment is accorded when the races are provided with substantially equal facilities, even though these facilities be separate. The 1953 decision, showing that the "separate but equal" standing of Negroes and others before the law rests on doctrine that is invalid, is a landmark decision which destroyed racial segregation in American law.

The social situation in the United States, as

Mr. Justice Hall noted, is very different from that in Canada in which the Drybones case arose, "but the basic philosophic concept is the same." Mr. Justice Hall went on: "The Canadian Bill of Rights is not fulfilled if it merely equates Indians with Indians in terms of equality before the law, but can have validity and meaning only when, subject to the single exception set out in s. 2 . . . , it is seen to repudiate discrimination in every law of Canada by reason of race, national origin, colour, religion or sex in respect of human rights and fundamental freedoms set out in s. 1 in whatever way that discrimination may manifest itself not only as between Indian and Indian but as between all Canadians whether Indian or non-Indian."

This pithy statement is the clearest and most concise summary of the Canadian Bill of Rights yet given in any of our courts. When I read the decision of the Supreme Court of Canada on the case of Joseph Drybones, I realized that a great precedent had been erected. The name of Joseph Drybones, an Indian of the Dogrib Band at Yellowknife in the Northwest Territories, may long be remembered by Canadians as they learn of the manner in which their liberties have broadened down, from precedent to precedent. My mind went back to the Dominion Day, July 1, 1960, when, as Prime Minister, I introduced the Canadian Bill of Rights in Parliament—the Bill that has broadened the rights and liberties of Joseph Drybones and many other Canadians. The practice of discrimination, I said, "above everything else in the world today" is an element of danger to the legions of freedom everywhere and to the nations that espouse freedom.

Referring to human rights and liberties, I said: "I defined them on one previous occasion as constituting the individual a sacred being and making him a sovereign in his dealing with the state. To adopt the words of that philosopher, Oliver Wendell Holmes of the United States Supreme Court, civil liberties give the right to the individual to hold the view that I disagree with so long as that individual keeps within the law and does not endeavour to undermine my beliefs by force.

"We have in effect today, although never adopted by Canada, a universal declaration of human rights which was passed by the United Nations. Its preamble sets forth clearly and unmistakably, as does the preamble of the United Nations Charter, the greatness of human rights and the determinant that the preservation of human rights is on the peace of the world. . . . This measure that I introduce is the first step on the part of Canada to carry out the acceptance of the international declaration of human rights."

I should like to add to that by recalling

something else I said when introducing the Bill of Rights, on that Dominion Day a dozen years ago. "It is one of those steps," I said, "which represent the achievement and the assurance of that degree of liberty and freedom under law that was envisaged by the Fathers of Confederation. I think it embodies a pledge to all Canadians, a pledge which I place before you not as something original but changed to meet the fact that I am speaking in the Canadian Parliament. I am a Canadian, a free Canadian, free to speak without fear, free to stand for what I think right, free to oppose what I believe wrong. This heritage of freedom I pledge to uphold for myself and all mankind."

7

On Becoming
a Freeman*

"To be of London is to share in a
stream of history that has enriched . . .
free men everywhere with the heritage
of the Common Law, trial by jury,
and parliamentary democracy."

*An address given at the Guild Hall on receiving the
freedom of the City of London, England, February
25, 1963.

Here in the heart of London, cradle of freedom in the Motherland of liberty and self-government, no man, least of all one from over the seas who has just "taken your Freedom", could fail to be touched by emotion or to be deeply grateful.

The Freedom of the City of London is a free gift, and the greatest civic distinction to which any man or woman can aspire.

It is the most cherished possession of many of the greatest personages in modern history. No one can demand it; no wealth can buy it; no power command it.

To be of London is to share in a stream of history that has enriched that quarter of the world's population within the Commonwealth, and free men everywhere, with the heritage . . . of the common law, trial by jury, and parliamentary democracy.

These are milestones and monuments of freedom for mankind in all parts of the world. And over all this, uniting each free community with the other, is the golden circle of the Crown. May Heaven bless and preserve it forever!

London is, as it has been for centuries, the most famous city in the world, with the testimony of deathless history in and all around it.

It is the symbol of the valour of the spirit of man in the cause of liberty. In that spirit your forebears wrested your Charter from the Conqueror in 1066; because of that spirit no conqueror has trod these streets since then.

And there is more in London's story than memoried greatness and old renown. Free men will never forget those fearful days of our own times when liberty was under siege in this city, when the men and women of this city matched the valour of freedom against regimented tyranny.

My Lord Mayor, I am privileged to accept the casket and all that it signifies, not only as a personal honour, but as a tribute to Canada and her people.

I thank you, Mr. Chamberlain, for the eloquent words you have spoken about me. That they are too generous for my merit I need hardly say. That they ever would be spoken was beyond the wildest flight of my imagination when I came to London for the first time as a junior officer in the Canadian Army in 1916. On many occasions since, I have returned, sometimes for personal, at other times for official, reasons.

I have come to know London in a way that might at least qualify me for the company of that celebrated person of whom we read in the *Pickwick Papers*: "Mr. Weller's knowledge of London was extensive — and peculiar."

Around us in this historic shrine are the figures and memorials of famous men of our common history and common heritage — men who in their day spoke the very proverbs of freedom.

History hastens to enshrine on its pages the fame and the glory of Sir Winston Churchill, already in life an immortal, who in a day when the waves broke over his island and no man could foresee the future, sent his winged words of defiance to strengthen the hearts and arms of free men everywhere, and more than any other man (or human force) ensured the victory.

Many of your famous men are as much a part of Canadian history as they are of yours. Time permits me to mention only the younger Pitt, who: "Finally fixed the British conception of the Cabinet as responsible to an independent House of Commons."

It was Pitt, on this very date, the 25th of February, in 1791, who introduced in your House of Commons the Quebec Government Bill, the principles of which are the cornerstone of the Canadian nationality.

Canada owes its being to the two founding races of Britain and France, and bilingualism and biculturalism within our country will always be a recognition of that historic fact. This bill brought the English and French together in unity by the creation of the two separate provinces of Upper and Lower Canada, and gave to our nation the beginnings of our parliamentary system. Indeed, history lived again, for centuries earlier had not the same two races, the Norman and Saxon, brought into being the first Parliament of England?

The debate which followed a few days after the introduction of the Quebec Government Bill was an historic one: for you, because during that debate occurred the rift between Burke and Fox; for us and for the other Commonwealth nations, because it established the principle that, as Fox put it, "the only means of retaining distant colonies with advantage is to enable them to govern themselves."

Around these walls are the coats of arms of all the famous City Guilds which gave leadership in colonizing distant lands.

In a very large measure these historic Livery companies remind us that it was trade and not conquest which carried the British flag to the ultimate seas.

Had it not been for trading organizations centred in London, there would have been no Commonwealth.

In the famous Guilds of the City of London are combined all those skills which have been in the past, and will continue to be, the source of trading and financial integrity throughout the world. Whatever the future may bring, I believe that through the glory of the past shines the promise of the future.

109

This city has been the centre of development in the past and may well provide the central initiative for a greater exchange of trade and finance which would give to the Commonwealth the role of world leadership at one time held by the Empire.

Without the example of a firmly founded municipal system of government, as has existed in this city for so long, it is unlikely that those who settled in far-off places in the pursuit of that trade would have perpetuated the British parliamentary and municipal systems, changed to meet the needs of local conditions.

Here in this place, with the representatives present of so many nations from all parts of the world, one cannot fail to refer to the Commonwealth.

The Commonwealth is an association of peoples even more than of governments. In it is the flowering of the seeds of the ideals of freedom, equality, and good government which were first planted, nurtured, and developed in this land and adapted to the needs of other lands to the ends of the earth.

Canada owes its being to its two founding nations — Britain and France.

It will ever be the pride of Canadians that the first success of the overseas adventure of British parliamentary government among Commonwealth nations took place in Canada. Many years in advance of its acceptance in the

United Kingdom, religious freedom was given to Canada by the British Parliament in 1774. The dignity of the human person was recognized in Canada when the first Parliament of Upper Canada in 1793 passed an act designed to abolish slavery.

Within fifteen years after the passing of the Reform Act of 1832, which firmly established Responsible Government in this land, that basic cornerstone of parliamentary democracy came to Canada "as a note in the pocket of a new Governor".

In 1867, under a Statute of the United Kingdom, Canada became the first self-governing Dominion under a federal system which has been changed or modified by other Commonwealth countries to meet their needs.

Confederation for Canada was a typical accomplishment of the British instinct for government meeting the needs of the democratic impatience of her peoples overseas. That process continues today to create new nations in many parts of the world.

The Commonwealth is the only proven pattern of mutual tolerance, understanding, and co-operation, whose principles show the pathway to a world at peace through goodwill among men.

The Commonwealth has not disintegrated as the sceptics have so often prophesied, but has flowered into the fullness of a free association of peoples such as the world has never seen.

Many trials and difficulties have had to be met. Others will arise.

Was it not Rossetti who asked, "Does the road wind uphill all the way?", and promptly answered: "Yes, to the very end."

These difficulties will be met, and I foresee a continuing expansion of the Commonwealth in the years ahead. Its base has been so broadened since the last war that no democratic nation which would desire to join us should or would be denied admission. This is the dream and the reality of the new Commonwealth.

In these last few years thirteen new nations have attained independence and have chosen to remain in the Commonwealth.

Two have left, and one elected not to join. Yet the peoples of these nations know that the light is still burning in the window. It may be that in the fullness of time they will join us in our faith that within the Commonwealth is to be found a political, economic, and spiritual ideology that in its principles, in brotherhood, and in co-operation, meets the needs and aspiration of the human soul.

"And from this hour
The hearts of brothers govern in our loves
And sway our great design."

As we go forward together there is work to

be done — internally, in the strengthening of the Commonwealth; externally, in bringing its influence to bear more and more on the problems of the world.

Conceived and born in London, an institution that has made a contribution to justice and freedom and to ever-rising economic standards among all its people, the Commonwealth has much unfinished business to do.

This is no hour for little aims and big fears. The Commonwealth needs to go forward in the things of the spirit in strength, for it has a mission for all mankind.

We must fully explore what can be done to expand trade within the Commonwealth as well as with all like-minded nations. We must expand the educational and cultural exchanges within the Commonwealth. We must produce greater designs for assistance to the underdeveloped countries within the Commonwealth.

We have our responsibilities as well outside our own fellowship.

In the last few years the united strength of the Commonwealth membership has espoused the great causes of the brotherhood of man, and the folly of the armaments race.

At the 1961 Conference of Prime Ministers we decided that racial discrimination as a policy was not compatible with the Commonwealth's abiding principles.

At the same Conference a joint and united

stand was taken for peace and disarmament by advocating abolition of both nuclear and conventional weapons and the establishment of a world authority for inspection and control. This was a forward step, being the first time in peace that the members of the Commonwealth have acted as a collective influence on world affairs.

My Lord Mayor, as I have already said, this day brings back to us the glory of our milestones and our memories.

How can we hold such memories in our hearts and not be moved?

Before us lies the far-flung community that God has built by your hands and the hands of its member nations everywhere in the world.

Shall we not resolve to strive to expand the concepts, for the good of all peoples, without difference of kind or race or origin? To strive for their freedom, for their right to lift themselves up from day to day and behold the things they have hoped for?

And may *we* not lift up *our* eyes to the great tracts of life yet to be conquered in the cause of righteous peace, of those yearnings which lie in the hearts of peoples and outlast all wars and errors of men?

I now come to the end, and so back to London, still as in the poet Cowper's day:

London, opulent, enlarged and still increasing London;

114

London, on whose river margent Canute bid
the waters to recede;
London, whose ancient privileges and free
customs were re-confirmed as long ago as
Runnymede.

London is, as Disraeli reminded us: "A nation,
not a City."

My Lord Mayor, I thank you from the heart
that I have been so honoured and am now a
Freeman of the greatest city of the world.

I can offer in return for so great an honour
and privilege only my humble and heartiest
gratitude.

And as your newest Honorary Freeman, I
pledge undying loyalty to one of your own
company, our most Gracious Queen, whom we
are proud to serve as The Queen of Canada.

8

Forward
to a World
Community*

"We are not here in this Assembly to
win wars of propaganda. We are
here to win victories for peace."

*An address at the United Nations General Assembly,
September 26, 1960.

Mr. President, I wish to congratulate you on your election. I know that the United Nations General Assembly will benefit greatly from your wisdom, experience, and independent judgment, qualities which are so essential in the discharge of those responsibilities that are yours; and may I add, sir, that one-tenth of Canada's population is of Irish origin, and they ask me to convey to you a particular word of congratulation.

I wish as well to join in welcoming the newly elected member states. I know that they will derive benefit and advantage from their membership in this organization, as the United Nations will benefit from their participation in its work and activities. It is particularly significant that thirteen of these new member states are in Africa, a continent in which great changes are taking place and which today holds the centre of the world's stage. I know all of us of the older members of this organization will agree that we have a responsibility to assist these new member states in solving the challenging problems with which they are faced.

Their addition to our membership is a reminder of the need for the Assembly to consider enlarging the Economic and Social Council and the numerical strength of the Security Council,

118

so that all geographical areas may receive adequate representation.

I wish now to speak of the present Assembly. To some observers the Assembly in the past week gave the appearance of being a circus and a drama of personalities. Whatever their views, this fact stands out, that this is the most important and most representative gathering of the world and national leaders in all history. This meeting symbolizes the bringing together of the cultures and philosophies of all races. It is our responsibility to ensure that out of this meeting shall come a testament to the capacity of rational men to achieve rational relations, to bring about the attainment of peace, and to practise brotherhood and the raising of standards everywhere in the world. To the new members I say this. As one representing Canada, I say that the United Nations constitutes the greatest hope for the middle and small powers, for the new and weaker states, indeed, for all the nations of mankind of every social and political system.

We meet under circumstances which, in my opinion, mean that this is a critical stage in the history and development of the United Nations. This organization faces its most formidable threat, a threat to its very existence. In the last few days the Assembly has heard from the leaders of its two most powerful members. I had great hopes when I learned that Mr.

Khrushchev was going to attend. I came here prepared to accept, to adopt, and to agree with any good suggestion he might offer, for I am of those who believe that his suggestions must not be rejected out of hand. I have been disappointed. Mr. Khrushchev, in a gigantic propaganda drama of destructive misrepresentation, launched a major offensive in the cold war. He gave lip-service to the United Nations which, in my opinion, would be destroyed by his proposal for a triumvirate. That speech could not have been intended to bring the world closer to peace; yet, to bring the world closer to peace is the major reason for our being here.

We do not always agree with the United States, but our very existence — with one-tenth of the population of the United States, and possessing the resources that we do — is an effective answer to the propaganda that the United States has aggressive designs. I say that to begin with President Eisenhower made a restrained, a wise, and a conciliatory speech. He presented a constructive program. He looked forward to a world community of peace. He opened the door to international conciliation and world fellowship. I am sorry to say that Mr. Khrushchev tried to shut that door.

This morning we heard from the Secretary General, the agent and trustee of this organization. I say at once that Canada rejects categorically the unjust and intemperate attacks

120

that have been made on the office and person of this wholly dedicated and impartial Secretary General. The proposal of the U.S.S.R. to replace the Secretary General with a three-man presidium requiring unanimous agreement to act is a transparent plan to undermine the prestige and authority of the United Nations. Having thwarted the United Nations so often through the exercise of the veto, the U.S.S.R. now seems bent on destroying the United Nations by neutralizing its power to proceed effectively and promptly in emergencies as they arise.

I need not add that Canada is opposed to that bizarre proposal; to accept it would require an amendment of the Charter; to accept it would be to reduce the United Nations to an instrument of indecision and impotence. It would, in fact, multiply the veto to the detriment of the effective operation of this organization.

I shall now say a few words on the Congo. What has happened there has given rise to one of the most challenging situations which the United Nations has ever had to face. I agreed with the Foreign Minister of Argentina when he pointed out that the results so far attained are a demonstration of what international co-operation can achieve when its members are determined to lend their full support.

Canada has played its part in United Nations

operations there; it did so at the request of the
United Nations, providing specially qualified
personnel — Signals, Communications, Air
Transport — and emergency food provisions.
Canada is a member of NATO. Is the fact that
we are a member of that defensive organization
any indication that the course we took, in providing this type of assistance on request, can be
described as being aggressive?

As I see it, one of the larger tasks of the
Assembly will be to ensure that sufficient support is forthcoming to sustain the United Nations in its efforts to revive the financial and
economic life of the Congo. I take this opportunity to assure the Assembly that Canada will
assume an equitable share of this burden.

I believe too that the experience in the Congo has demonstrated the need to have military
forces readily available for service with the
United Nations when required. For its part the
Canadian government has held in reserve a bat-
talion, transportable by air, and earmarked for
such service. That experience in the Congo has
emphasized, as I see it, the need for the
establishment under the United Nations of the
nucleus of a permanent headquarters military
staff to be in readiness to prevent confusion
and to assure cohesion when called upon in an
emergency.

Canada's views on the Congo and on the
larger African problem may be summarized in

this way. The African continent must not become the focus of an East-West struggle; it must be free from the direct interference of the major powers. The African nations must be permitted to work out their own destinies; when they need help, the best source is through the agencies of the United Nations.

I turn now to a subject dealt with at great length by the Chairman of the Council of Ministers of the U.S.S.R., the subject of colonialism. He asked for and advocated a declaration at this session for *"the complete and final elimination of colonial regimes"*. I think it would be generally agreed that, whatever the experience of the past, there can no longer be a relationship of master and servant anywhere in the world. He has spoken of colonial bondage, of exploitation, and of foreign yokes. Those views, uttered by the master of the major colonial power in the world today, followed the admission of fourteen new member nations to the United Nations — all of them former colonies. It seems that he forgot what had occurred on the opening day.

Since the last war seventeen colonial areas and territories, comprising more than forty million people, have been brought to complete freedom by France. In the same period fourteen colonies and territories, comprising half a billion people, have achieved complete freedom within the Commonwealth. Taken together,

123

some 600 million people in more than thirty
countries, most of them now represented in this
Assembly, have attained their freedom — this
with the approval, the encouragement, and the
guidance of the United Nations, the Commonwealth, and France. There are few here that
can speak with the authority of Canada on the
subject of colonialism, for Canada was once a
colony of both France and the United Kingdom. We were the first country which evolved,
over a hundred years ago, by constitutional
processes from colonial status to independence
without severing the family connection.

The Commonwealth now embraces ten
nations, including the United Kingdom, all of
them free and voluntary members from all the
continents, comprising one-fifth of the world's
population and representing virtually every
race, colour, and creed. We are united not by
the sword or the seal but by the spirit of co-
operation and by common aspirations; and the
process is a continuing one. Within the next
week another country, Nigeria, the most
populous in Africa, will attain its independence
and remain in the Commonwealth family.

Indeed, in this Assembly the membership is
composed in a very considerable measure of
the graduates of empires, mandates, and
trusteeships of the United Kingdom, the Commonwealth, and other nations. I pause to ask
this question: *"How many human beings have*

been liberated by the U.S.S.R.?" Do we forget
how one of the postwar colonies of the
U.S.S.R. sought to liberate itself four years ago,
and with what results? I say that because these
facts of history in the Commonwealth and
other countries invite comparison with the
domination over peoples and territories, sometimes gained under the guise of liberation, but
always accompanied by the loss of political
freedom. How are we to reconcile the tragedy
of the Hungarian uprising in 1956 with Chairman Khrushchev's confident assertion of a few
days ago in this Assembly? Mr. Khrushchev
said: "It has been and always will be our stand
that the peoples of Africa, like those of other
continents striving for their liberation from the
colonial yoke, should establish orders in their
countries of their own will and choice. . ."
That I accept — and I hope that those words
mean a change of attitude for the future on the
part of those he represents.

What of Lithuania, Estonia, Latvia? What of
the freedom-loving Ukrainians, and many other
Eastern European peoples which I shall not
name for fear of omitting some of them? Mr.
Khrushchev went further and said: "Complete
and final elimination of the colonial regime
in all its forms and manifestations has been
prompted by the entire course of world history
in the last decades . . ."

There can be no double standard in interna-

tional affairs. I ask the Chairman of the Council of Ministers of the U.S.S.R. to give to those nations under his domination the right of free elections — to give them the opportunity to determine the kind of government they want under genuinely free conditions. If those conclusions were what his words meant, for they must apply universally, then indeed will there be new action to carry out the obligations of the United Nations Charter; then indeed will there be new hope for all mankind.

My hope is that those words of his will be universally acceptable and that he will give the lead towards their implementation here and now.

I wish now to say a few words on East-West relations. A year ago we had great hopes. There seemed to be a promise of a decisive change in relations among the great powers. We, the smaller powers and the middle powers, find ourselves in the position of trying to make our contribution to removing fear and distrust, to bringing about mutual understanding and cooperation. The Ten-Nation Committee began its work. Until the failure of even the opening of the Summit Conference, there were high expectations. Then came the collapse of that Conference. Then there was the withdrawal of the U.S.S.R. from the disarmament negotiations in June. Then came those propaganda attacks during this summer in degree and intensity, the very violence of which must naturally lead to the view that various issues were being deliberately exploited for the express purpose of raising tension. With mankind waiting for us to act, what good can come from threats to rain rockets or nuclear bombs on other countries, large or small, to dispatch so-called volunteers into situations already dangerously inflamed, to encourage political leaders to follow the line of extremism? Mankind, the peoples of all the nations, are fearful and anxious, and these fears and anxieties aggravate the tensions. I ask for a return immediately to the path of negotiation. It is the only course that the great powers should follow. It is incumbent on this United Nations General Assembly to press for the resumption of negotiations, particularly regarding those main issues which divide the U.S.S.R. and those associated with it from the western powers. That is the paramount issue of this Assembly, disarmament. The Canadian Government takes its stand on behalf of full disarmament, to be assured by effective control and inspection. The major powers today possess the nuclear capacity for mutual destruction, and to annihilate all. We, the middle powers and the smaller powers, cannot remain silent. We would be the hopeless victims of any nuclear catastrophe that takes place. Quite apart from our instinct for self-preservation, mankind knows of the futility of wanton waste. Without a return to negotiations, we cannot hope to arrest the arms race, we cannot hope to still the process of continuing armaments.

The tragedy of the Ten-Power negotiations was that the breakdown occurred at a time when there was an appreciable narrowing of the gap between the Soviet and Western positions. I wrote to Mr. Khrushchev on June 30. I suggested then a return to the negotiating table. The unanimous voice of the disarmament commission in that regard has been disregarded, for in August it called for the earliest possible continuance of disarmament negotiations. I believe that it is imperative for this Assembly to reaffirm the appeal of the disarmament commission.

It is not plans and principles which we need. We have four different disarmament plans and two sets of principles. There may be working methods that should be brought about, to be adjusted by agreement. Canada suggested the appointment of a neutral chairman, and is prepared to examine every constructive suggestion. We do not lack appropriate machinery but we do lack mutual confidence and a general will on the part of the Soviet Government to negotiate.

That confidence can be increased by dispelling the kind of secrecy which clouds preparations for war and fills the hearts of men with fear of surprise attack. Canada is the nearest neighbour of the U.S.A. and the U.S.S.R. Our people fear, and the people of the U.S.A. fear, a surprise attack across the polar regions. No doubt the people of the U.S.S.R fear an attack from our side. Canada is prepared to make available for international inspection and control, any part of Canadian Arctic territory in exchange for a comparable concession on the part of the U.S.S.R. They say that we prepare, in co-operation with the U.S.A. in our Arctic areas, to attack. I give them the opportunity now to have an answer to their fears. You open your areas, and we will open ours, and that source of fear will be removed.

I find it difficult to understand, if it was reported correctly, why Mr. Khrushchev should have taken the view the day before yesterday that a resumption of disarmament talks should be conditional, among other things, upon the acceptance of demands by the U.S.S.R. for fundamental changes in the Ten-Power Committee and in the office of the Chief Executive of the United Nations.

What other kind of measures might be undertaken? I have frequently had occasion to urge publicly the end of nuclear weapons, the systematic control of missiles designed to deliver nuclear weapons of mass destruction, the designation and inspection of launching sites for missiles, the abolition of biological and chemical weapons, the outlawing of outer space for military purposes and, especially, a ban on the mounting of armaments on orbital satellites, an end to the production of fissionable materials for weapons, and the conversion of existing stocks for peaceful purposes. Canada over and over again has advocated an end to nuclear testing.

I need hardly stress the significance of early agreement on measures like these, carried out under appropriate verifications and inspection, for there can be no dissipation of fear unless there is control and inspection. Tremendous advances have been made in outer space. It will be too late a year from now. I hope that at this time consideration will be given to the assurance that jurisdiction in outer space be for scientific and peaceful purposes only, so that all nations, great and small, will have equal rights.

I believe, and Canada takes the stand, that no celestial body shall be considered as capable of appropriation by any state; that space vehicles shall be identified by a system of registration of launchings, call signs, and other characteristics; that frequencies for communications with and among space vehicles shall be allocated on a rational and agreed basis.

These tremendous problems require the consideration of the United Nations Committee on the peaceful uses of outer space — and that body should commence its work at once.

I should like to say a word too on the subject of aid and assistance. While the Chairman of the Council of Ministers dwelt at length on the evils of colonialism, he had very little to say about economic assistance to the less-developed countries of the world. I read no pledge to make increased contributions to the United Nations programs of economic and technical assistance. That was one view expressed by President Eisenhower. Mr. Khrushchev asked simply for a declaration.

There is an urgent need to increase the flow of international economic aid to the less-developed countries, and I think particularly of these newly independent states of Africa. I believe this: Through the United Nations the material resources for economic assistance must be greatly increased if the needs of Africa are to be met without impairing at the same time plans for assistance in other areas. We in Canada have taken one stand in this regard. We have given economic and technical assistance. We do not condone the imposition upon recipient nations of any particular social, economic, or political order. We will maintain our contributions to aid programs. We will make increases.

Canada naturally has a family concern for

those countries achieving independence within the Commonwealth of Nations. Last week, the Special Commonwealth African Aid Programme was publicly launched. For this purpose Canada will, subject to parliamentary sanction, make a contribution of $10.5 million over three years towards the development of African countries within the Commonwealth, including some of the dependent territories. There will be technical assistance and aids to education under this plan, and assistance in the field of capital investment. We regard bilateral assistance within the Commonwealth as complementary to the United Nations program in Africa and we will take every means to ensure that bilateral aid is closely co-ordinated with the United Nations programs. To the International Bank of Reconstruction and Development we have doubled our subscription. We have made financial provision for a contribution to the International Development Association. We believe that the United Nations Special Fund and the expanded program of technical assistance deserve to have increased contributions. The specific amounts of these contributions will be announced by the Canadian delegation during this session of the United Nations.

One of these — the OPEX program — has proved its effectiveness in providing much-needed assistance to new countries. We think it should be made permanent and expanded.

We place before you a complementary proposal to establish a roster. We intend, in Canada, to establish a roster of Canadian experts in various fields — ready at short notice to be sent under United Nations auspices to newly independent states requesting them. They can help in setting up or restoring civil administration such as in the Congo, in distress areas, or in disaster areas. National action of a stand-by nature is obviously desirable to supplement the United Nations OPEX proposal. We suggest that experts, in an experts' bank, if you will, might be recruited for medicine, public health, sanitation, public welfare, distribution of supplies, communications, transportation, and police services. To set up an expert bank would make for administrative stability instead of having to rely on a crash recruiting campaign for this purpose after the need arises.

One matter which Canada has pressed in the past, and which I now repeat, is in the field of providing aid through food contributions. The problem of feeding the millions of chronically hungry and undernourished people of the world is tragic and urgent. Some of our countries have tremendous surpluses of cereals and other foodstuffs. We also have the capacity to increase our production greatly. Canada's surplus of wheat, as of July 31, was 536 million bushels. Surplus food, piled up in sterile storage, is hard to justify when so many human beings lack adequate food and nutrition. I realize, as the Food and Agriculture Organization has stated, that agricultural surpluses of the more advanced countries would be only temporary relief and would be therefore incomplete. I believe, however, that much must be done on behalf of food-deficit countries, first to help them in their hour of need, and then to help them raise their own levels of production. This to me is the responsibility of the United Nations as a whole, to meet this challenge.

A few countries cannot underwrite the costs of transferring their surpluses to the countries in need. What we need is to join together in contributing to a solution of truly world-wide scope to this problem of the world's suffering and starving peoples. We have tried to do that.

We have no ambitions internationally. We covet no country. We want to change no country's views. We have made available, in wheat and flour to under-developed countries, aid in the amount of $56 million. I now welcome and commend the suggestion made by the President of the United States last week that the Assembly should seriously consider devising a workable plan along the lines of the "Food for Peace" program. We envisage a "food bank" to provide food to member states through the

United Nations. Such a scheme would require the establishment of concerted machinery which would take into account established patterns of trade and marketing, and co-ordinate the individual surplus disposal to improve the effective utilization of wheat.

Finally, for some reason, we have never been able to secure agreement on the compulsory authority of the International Court of Justice — that is, the judicial arm of the United Nations — in the strengthening of peace-keeping machinery. The compulsory jurisdiction of the International Court, in the opinion of the country I represent, is of paramount importance. All members of the United Nations are automatically parties to the statute. Canada accepts the compulsory jurisdiction of the Court except in matters of a domestic nature, but does not itself decide what is of a domestic nature, and leaves it to the Court to decide. I hope that the nations in this Organization will declare their readiness to accept the Court's compulsory jurisdiction so as to give sinew and muscle to the decisions that are made.

I have spoken for Canada. We are, as I have said, a middle power, large enough to bear responsibility but not so large as to have traditions of national power, or aspirations which arouse fears and suspicion. As a nation of North America, we have our deep roots in two European cultures — the British and the

French — and also in the cultures of all the other races of men that have come to us.

By the accident of geography and history we find ourselves squarely between the two greatest powers on earth. We have no fortresses facing either. We want to live at peace with our northern neighbours, as we have lived so long at peace with our southern neighbours.

In a world passing through two great human experiences — the thrust of technology and the thrust of political and social change — new perspectives have been given for a better life. Must we admit that we cannot control these revolutions of science and society? Shall we rather harness them for the common good, do it now, and prevent them from upsetting the all-too-fragile foundations on which peace rests today? That is our task. We hear voices that speak of victories for propaganda. We are not here in this Assembly to win wars of propaganda. We are here to win victories for peace. If I understand correctly the thinking of the average man and woman today throughout the world, they have had enough of propaganda, of confusion, and fears, and doubts. They are asking us for the truth. We are not mustered here under the direction and dominiation of any nation. We are mustered not for any race or creed or ideology. We are here for the hosts of humanity everywhere in the world. Peoples and nations are waiting upon us. Man's hopes call upon us to say what we can do. My hope is that we shall not leave this place without having done something for mankind, so that we shall be able to say to the peoples of the world that death's pale flag shall not again be raised in war, that fear shall be lifted from the hearts and souls of men. For this could be our last chance to achieve those objectives.

9

One Canada, One Nation*

"Are we to have one or two degrees of
citizenship in the two Canadas?
Canada was divided into two nations
between 1841 and 1867.
It was the failure of that concept that
brought about Confederation."

*The speech given to the Progressive Conservative
Convention at Toronto in September 1967.

Almost eleven years ago, I was honoured with the highest position that can come to anyone in the Progressive Conservative party. Tonight I intend to review, but shortly, something of the story of those eleven years. Then I shall place before you some ideas regarding policies for this nation, which in my opinion, are necessary and without which we, as a nation, can never attain the destiny that ought to be ours.

This is the message that I give you today — "Le Canada français a besoin du Canada; le Canada a besoin du Canada français." That has been my attitude throughout the years.

We are a party with a great tradition, a party of great principles. In this convention, we hold communion with those who have gone before. We change not principles, we change programs to meet modern conditions, using as a basis principles which brought this party into existence. These principles have served our country before and since Confederation. Our purpose must be to leave a memorial of greatness to future generations.

I say today, as I said eleven years ago, "This is a time for greatness." National unity requires it. The cause of freedom demands it. This is an occasion when this nation calls for

Canada first; one Canada. That was Macdonald's objective. That has been mine through the years.

I have marched in the ranks of this party since 1917. Yet, until 1957, only once (in 1930) did we win an election nationally. What I have tried to do over the years and since being chosen leader of the party is to bring together the people of all the races of men, to make it a people's party, a party of all Canadians. We had widespread support in the last general election. How many of you realize this fact — that in 1965, out of the millions of votes that were cast, if, in twenty constituencies, we had secured 11,300 votes more, we would be the government of Canada today?

When we came into office in 1957, not one member of our Cabinet had even seen the Cabinet room. We had been out of office so long that we had almost an exemplification of eternity. We ended that. In the last two election campaigns, we elected the largest number of members the Conservative Party has ever had, when in opposition, in all its history.

We have today a clearer title, because of our past principle and tradition, and a stronger obligation, to preserve national unity than in the last hundred years. Let us draw on the spiritual wells of our past in solving the problems of the present. Cartier and Macdonald said this

141

was one nation. They stood, their memory stands, for a united Canada.

In the last four years, we have seen a Government "frittering around" in their relations with the provinces. They brought about what they called "co-operative federalism". It was neither co-operative nor federalism. They promised to meet with the provinces "eye to eye" — "eyeball to eyeball"! And, ever since, they have substituted "chin to chin". In capitulation to promises they brought about opting-out, two pensions plans, two flags, two student loan plans. They have even, by unification of the armed forces, opted out of the defence of this nation! What are they building? Ten separate governments with vast authority? To Quebec, they have promised everything under the sun. They have opted this out and opted that out. It's time that French Canada started opting in rather than opting out.

They brought in the concept of "two nations" in the Prime Minister's speech after taking office in 1963. The object of Confederation was not to produce Siamese twins in this nation. What has happened? Differences, difficulties, divisions on every hand. The major policies: we brought them about and they criticized them; they follow them today. They have squandered the taxpayer's money, and are spending ten million dollars a day more today than we did during the last year of our administration. A few days ago, when dealing with pressing problems of unity, the economy, inflation, and other matters, the Prime Minister said: "I'm not disturbed." "Do not disturb" is all right as a slogan on a hotel room but it doesn't represent leadership for Canada. The other day he said, in a casual, off-hand way, "I'm not disturbed. Higher taxes a r e inevitable." And then he explained this away by saying it was anti-pollution measures that brought the situation about. The readiest and least expensive measure of that kind that I can think of would be to get rid of the present government at the earliest possible date.

Now I am going to speak of principles and policies. Principles are the heart and soul of the party. Policies divorced from principles are dangerous. One question propounded earlier this evening was "Which way should the party go?" Some say we should go the way of reaction. Some, who have been trying to make policies for the party in an off-stage chorus, say we should follow the course taken by Senator Goldwater and the Republican Party in 1964.

There is criticism, generally confined to Liberal ranks, against the Monarchy. It has become popular among some Canadians to malign Canada's heritage. They argue that the past is dead. Much has been done by the present government to deprecate the Monarchy,

143

to remove traditional symbols, to play games with the coat of arms, to unify our armed forces and get rid of uniforms that show Canada's British tradition. I say to my friends in French Canada: the freedom you enjoy in our country came because there was a British monarchial system. Our leaders believed it was the only way Canada could ensure its independence. They opposed republicanism, what they called "American domination". They decided to build a Canada here, Canada first, foremost, and always. So to each of you, I say I believe in Canada — a Canada undivided. A Canadian I was born, a Canadian I will die. That paraphrases the attitude taken by Macdonald. When in office, we maintained the Constitution, we equalized opportunities in the various provinces, we developed northern Canada, we entered into the greatest development plan this nation had ever seen, we abolished discrimination under the law. We stood for one Canada.

Down through the years, Canadians of other racial origins than the parent races, English and French, generally were not supporters of this party. They are today because they have a Bill of Rights that protects them against discrimination. They are with us today. The Liberal Party has, by its two-nations policy, placed these people in a second-class, secondary position as citizens and we ought not to follow suit.

We expanded social security. We thought of the veteran, the older people, the sick, and the crippled. I was criticized for being too much concerned with the average Canadians. I can't help that; I am one of them! My thoughts have been with the under-privileged and the afflicted. I have no apologies to offer for I believe in the words of the Scripture that read, "Thou shalt open thine hand wide unto thy brother, to thy poor, and to thy needy, in thy land."

We gave the young men and women of this nation an opportunity for technological training that has never been equalled in any other nation, but which is being discontinued by the present government. What about the marvellous Canadian record in sportsmanship in the last couple of world or international athletic events? We set up a Fitness Council to encourage amateur sport. When in power, we gave young Canadians opportunities, we raised standards, we gave them new hope — hope that they in this nation under free enterprise, protected against injustice, would be able to make their full contribution in their day and generation.

We did something more. We ended discrimination. I refused over the years to join any club that practised discrimination on the basis of colour or religion. Through the years I acted for the Indians and we were able to give them their rights for the first time. In the Prime

Ministers' Conference in London, in 1960 and 1961, I was for a time alone in the stand that I took. I said, "This Commonwealth, with five out of six belonging to a coloured race, cannot, dare not, be other than colour blind." And today that principle is accepted in the Commonwealth.

Now I want to speak particularly to French Canada. I have never been unmindful of French Canada, of its heritage, its courage, and its devotion. If it had not been for your ancestors and forebears in 1776, there would be no Canada today. You stood. You stood in 1812. Without your participation one hundred years ago, there would have been no Confederation.

Recognition of the two cultures, of the parent races, was and must remain the very base of Confederation. It was because we believed that, that I recommended the appointment of a French-speaking Governor General. My administration made it possible, by simultaneous translation in the House of Commons, to make Parliament bilingual. We appointed a fair share of French Canadians for the first time in senior positions in the civil service, in foreign affairs, and on boards. We settled the university grants problem. Yes, and we brought Expo to Canada. We tried to convene a national confederation conference for Canada to settle the constitutional problem but we were defeated before the meeting could be convened.

I am going to make an appeal to you and your conscience. The rights of Canadians, whether of the parent races or otherwise, must not be placed on the auction block for political gain, or to use a colloquialism, "put up for grabs".

I stood against the Prime Minister when he announced the "two nations" idea. Laurier said it was wrong, Macdonald said it was wrong, Cartier said it was wrong, and every Prime Minister and leading French-speaking representative throughout the years has said it was wrong. They didn't believe in two nations. They didn't believe in a state within a state, or an associate state. Today, the Liberals and the N.D.P. between them have appropriated support for one or both of these propositions. They have raised the bidding on constitutional problems, politically, to fantastic heights. You may not agree with me, but the theory that Canada is two nations can only lead to division and dissension and finally to de-Confederation. If you bring it into effect, what about the six million Canadians of racial origins other than the parent races? Are they to have second-class citizenship? I shall never agree with that. Are we to have degrees of citizenship? Through the years (and it is fifty years since I first spoke on this subject; I had just come out of the armed forces and was proud of the Canada badge on

my shoulder strap.) I have said, "Let us be
Canadians." That has been the course I have
followed throughout the years. Are we to have
degrees of citizenship? Are we to have one or
two degrees of citizenship in two Canadas?
Canada was divided into two nations between
1841 and 1867. It was the failure of that concept that brought about Confederation. Macdonald, Cartier, Brown, and all the other
Fathers of Confederation agreed that, to meet
this failure, confederation into one nation was
the solution.

The adoption of the two-nations concept
would segregate French Canada. I am not going
to argue whether it's popular or not, to take this
stand, to erect a Berlin Wall around the Province of Quebec. That is what this proposition
will do. Its proponents say that to understand it
requires knowledge of the meaning of "nation";
that while it is the same word in both
languages, the meaning of "two nations" is different in French and in English. Laurier said,
"This is one nation." Cartier said "This is one
nation." Langevin, Bourassa, St. Laurent said
the same, all through the years. We are asked
today to go back to the period between 1841
and 1867, to two Canadas. I plead with you
not to accept a "watered-down" version of
Liberal or N.D.P. policy. This party cannot
walk forward to that new Canada when Canadians, whatever their racial origin, are equal if

the Conservative Party starts on the course of walking backwards to 1841, or being dragged back to the days of Louis XIV.

I would like to have spoken at length on this because I am pleading with you. I am looking into the hearts of Canadians everywhere. I know what discrimination is. I know how much easier it would have been for me if my name had been Bannerman, which was my mother's name. But from the earliest days when equality was unpopular, I raised the standard of equality in this country. Let us be Canadians. Let us not deny equality to those whose surnames are not of the parent races. I don't believe that the true heart of French Canada wants the two-nations idea. It is a minority who yell so loud they give the impression of being a majority. In the last week, I have had many letters from the Province of Quebec in opposition to the two-nations idea. The two-nations proposition is dangerous to Quebec. It is destructive of its best interests. It will establish a reserve. I am against discrimination. Don't let this party turn back to the period 1841 to 1867. We dare not consider the possibility of Quebec's being ushered or opted out of Canada. We don't want any "check-point Charlies" in this country.

There are many other issues. In 1957 I promised French Canada their constitutional rights and they got them. But I do not promise, and no party has the right to promise, to add any additional rights without agreement by the peoples of all the provinces. It was because I believed this that invitations were sent out, in February 1963, to convene a constitutional conference. We were defeated before the conference met. The scope of the conference would have included the study of means to patriate the Constitution. I belong to those who believe that we ought to write the Constitution anew, and that it should be done by Canadians, for Canadians, and in Canada. But we haven't arrived at that point yet. The constitutional convention would have dealt with national symbols. It would not have given us a flag with no heritage. It would have examined the areas of disagreement within the nation. It would have re-stated the goals of Confederation for the next hundred years. It would have endeavoured to bar prejudices and misunderstanding, and it wouldn't — as this two-nations proposition will — place Canadians of other racial origins in a secondary position. Liberalism has done that. Is the Conservative Party to become a slavish ape of a policy that is dangerous to Canada?

I stand here today in the city of Toronto to which a hundred and fifty years ago my ancestors came. My boyhood was spent in East York. I have nostalgic memories of Todmorden and Don Mills Road. I looked ahead in my boyhood to doing my part to build in Canada a citizenship that would allow equality to those of us who are not, in our surnames, of the two parent races.

This party has given me everything. To those who have given me their loyalty and support, there are no words to express my feelings. We weren't always right. One time an Ontario leader came to Macdonald and said "You know, Sir John, I'm always with you when you are right." Sir John told him where he might go. "What I need is people who are with me when we're wrong," said Sir John. In democracy, you can't always be right. But you can be honest. I am asked — and I am speaking to young Canada now — are there any rewards in public life? There are — not monetary but there is a tremendous satisfaction in being able to say "I tried, I stood."

A leader has to take responsibility. He has to have courage. It is easy to point out the easy road. I could have done that on the subject of nuclear proliferation. In 1963 I refused to sanction proliferation, and today that policy is accepted internationally. I have never asked for sympathy, nor do I now. Leaders have to take action which they believe will serve the nation. Is there any reward while one lives? I wish you could read my correspondence, my letters from across this nation in the last week or so. Humble people who generally do not speak out

151

have written and sent telegrams. Their sentiments cannot be purchased.

I followed this party when I didn't agree with all of its policies because the disagreement of one person or another does not mean the policy isn't right; and I gave loyalty to leader after leader because I believe that there is no other way for a party to be able to carry out its responsibilities.

Canada faces a crisis the gravity of which calls for statesmanship. I must tell you, in all frankness and without equivocation, I cannot accept the two-nations policy. I implore you. You will make that decision for me when you decide on that policy, because I cannot and shall not accept it. I am not going to go back a hundred years and more to borrow a policy that has proven to be wrong, to get votes in 1967. The subcommittee and committee on policy have accepted the two-nations principle. I hope that the Convention will repudiate it before we leave here. I cannot be interested in the question of leadership in this party under a policy that is borrowed from Liberalism. Accept two nations and you will destroy the tremendous advances of the last few years, in bringing to this party Canadians of so many races.

We are in a national crisis. National goals will never be attained by following uncertain courses designed to secure immediate advantage. I believe in compromise, even infinite compromise, provided that it is based on principle, compassion, and toleration. But I will not compromise with what is wrong or capitulate to the vociferous clamour of the few who believe that they are going to take a Liberal policy that is all but discredited, and borrow it at a time the Liberal Party is running away from it as fast as it can, or the diluted one of the N.D.P. with special status.

Canada needs a renewed sense of national purpose. We need to maintain and to strengthen the basic foundations of our constitution. We need to instil in every Canadian the spirit of Sir George Etienne Cartier. "Before all let's be Canadians."

It is my purpose in life to maintain the basic foundation of the Constitution, to make the diversity of our national origin a source of pride to all; to have Canadians realize the richness of its many cultures. Men and women of this Convention! Don't move backwards. There is no one who can show me that suddenly, in 1967, "nation" in French means something different from what it means in English. Laurier didn't say that. St. Laurent didn't say that. Cartier didn't. Bourassa didn't. They used "nation" in both languages as synonyms. I could not accept any leadership that carries with it this policy that denies everything that I have stood for throughout life. Some say,"Oh, it's easy to do that. All you do is say the words don't mean the same thing". If the words don't mean anything, why change them? If this doesn't mean anything, why do it? Whom are you trying to fool? It is just an example of word culture — if that is what they say — it doesn't mean anything — then why bring it in and divide this nation and divide this party

What has the nation done for an ordinary person like me? What can it do for those who are prepared to devote themselves? Your Canada, my Canada. I give you a line from a young Canadian poet, Stephen Smith, who died in Montreal in 1964. He left a memorable line worthy of Rupert Brooke, "Canada should be a reflection of God's eyes". Let us unite. Let us end this business of trying to bring about a policy that will destroy. Let us bring about one nation, one that is undivided. Let us bind the nation in unity and heal the wounds of division.

My dedication is simple. Whatever remains to me of life, be it long or short (they have been predicting my demise politically and personally for many years, and I am still here), whatever remains to me of life — Almighty God has been bountiful to me — I will give to the service of my country. I will continue to fight for those things that I have fought for throughout life. Some say, Let us go back to the good old days. I was there at that time. Not one Conservative from Quebec in 1921; in 1935, five; in 1940, none; in 1945, two; and in 1949, three. And then they say there's something wrong with Diefenbaker because he has more seats today than three leaders had in four elections.

Ladies and gentlemen, there is my dedication.

Paraphrasing the words of one who gave leadership in his day and generation, may all of us in this Convention and across Canada join a great cathedral of dedication, not to party, but first to Canada, to the Canada we love. "May we all in words speak wisdom, in thought show faith, in life give service, and in death show courage."

Appendix

The Drybones Judgment:
A landmark for freedom in Canada

Ten years after the Parliament of Canada enacted the Bill of Rights providing that human rights and fundamental freedoms shall exist without discrimination by reason of race, national origin, colour, religion, or sex, a case bearing upon this great principle reached the Supreme Court of Canada. A charge of drunkenness in a public place had been laid against Joseph Drybones, a Dogrib Indian of Yellowknife, Northwest Territories, under the Indian Act, which provided more severe penalties than those specified in liquor laws under which non-Indians would be charged. Drybones was acquitted on the ground that conviction would impair his rights under the Bill of Rights. The Supreme Court upheld his acquittal, its judgment being written by Mr. Justice Ritchie. An edited text of that judgment follows.

157

HER MAJESTY THE QUEEN
v.
JOSEPH DRYBONES

This is an appeal brought with leave of this Court from a judgment of the Court of Appeal for the Northwest Territories dismissing an appeal by the Crown from a judgment of Mr. Justice W. G. Morrow of the Territorial Court of the Northwest Territories by which he had acquitted Joseph Drybones of being "unlawfully intoxicated off a reserve" contrary to the *Indian Act,* after having heard an appeal by way of trial *de novo* from a judgment of Magistrate Anderson-Thompson who had convicted the respondent of this offence and sentenced him to be fined $10.00 and costs and in default to spend three days in custody.

The respondent is an Indian and he was indeed intoxicated on the evening of April 8th, 1967, on the premises of the Old Stope Hotel in Yellowknife in the Northwest Territories where there is no "reserve" within the meaning of the *Indian Act.*

When he was first arraigned before Magistrate Anderson-Thompson, Drybones, who spoke no English, pleaded guilty to this offence, but on appeal to the Territorial Court, Mr. Justice Morrow found that there was some serious doubt as to whether he fully appreciated his plea in the lower court and he was allowed to withdraw that plea whereafter the appeal proceeded as a trial *de novo* with a plea of not guilty. Section 94 of the *Indian Act* reads as follows:

> 94. An Indian who
> (a) has intoxicants in his possession,
> (b) is intoxicated, or
> (c) makes or manufactures intoxicants off a reserve, is guilty of an offence and is liable on summary conviction to a fine of not less than ten dollars and not more than fifty dollars or to imprisonment for a term not exceeding three months or to both fine and imprisonment.

I agree with the Court of Appeal that the use of the words "off a reserve" creates

> ... an essential element to be proved in any charge laid under section 94. But once it is proved, as it was in the present case, that the offence was not committed upon a reserve, the requirement of the section was satisfied. The fact that there are no reserves in the Territories is quite irrelevant.

The important question raised by this appeal has its origin in the fact that in the Northwest Territories it is not an offence for anyone except an Indian to be intoxicated otherwise than in a public place. The Liquor Ordinance which is of general application in the Territories, provides that:

> No person shall be in an intoxicated condition in a public place . . .

but unlike s.94 of the *Indian Act,* there is no provision for a minimum fine and the maximum term of imprisonment is only 30 days as opposed to 3 months under the *Indian Act.*

The result is that an Indian who is intoxicated in his own home "off a reserve" is guilty of an offence and subject to a minimum fine of not less than $10 or a term of imprisonment not exceeding 3 months or both, whereas all other citizens in the Territories may, if they see fit, become intoxicated otherwise than in a public place without committing any offence at all. And even if any such other citizen is convicted of being intoxicated in a public place, the only penalty provided by the Ordinance is "a fine not exceeding $50 or . . . imprisonment for a term not exceeding 30 days or . . . both fine and imprisonment."

The argument which was successfully advanced by the respondent before Mr. Justice Morrow and before the Court of Appeal was that because of this legislation, Indians in the Northwest Territories, by reason of their race, are denied "equality before the law" with their fellow Canadians, and that s.94(b) of the *In-*

dian Act therefore authorizes the abrogation, abridgment or infringement of one of the human rights and fundamental freedoms recognized and declared as existing in Canada without discrimination by reason of race, pursuant to the *Canadian Bill of Rights*, which provides:

1.   It is hereby recognized and declared that in Canada there have existed and shall continue to exist without discrimination by reason of race, national origin, colour, religion or sex, the following human rights and fundamental freedoms, namely, . . .

> (b) the right of the individual to equality before the law and the protection of the law;

2.   Every law of Canada shall, unless it is expressly declared by an Act of Parliament of Canada that it shall operate notwithstanding the Canadian Bill of rights, be so construed and applied as not to abrogate, abridge or infringe, or to authorize the abrogation, abridgment or infringement of any of the rights or freedoms herein recognized and declared . . .

5.   (2) The expression "law of Canada" in Part I means an Act of the Parliament of Canada enacted before or after the coming into force of this Act, any order, rule or regulation thereunder, and any law in force in Canada or in any part of

Canada at the commencement of this Act
that is subject to be repealed, abolished or
altered by the Parliament of Canada.

The Court of Appeal agreed with Mr. Justice
Morrow that s.94(b) of the *Indian Act* is rendered inoperative by reason of this legislation . . .

It was contended on behalf of the appellant
that the reasoning and conclusion of the courts
below makes the question of whether s.94 has
been rendered inoperative by the *Bill of Rights*
dependent upon whether or not the law of any
province or territory makes it an offence to be
intoxicated otherwise than in a public place and
that its operation could therefore not only vary
from place to place in Canada but also from
time to time, depending upon amendments
which might be made to the provincial or territorial legislation. I can, however, find no
room for application of this argument in the
present case as the ordinance in question is a
law of Canada within the meaning of the *Bill of
Rights*, and it is a law of general application in
the Territories, whereas the *Indian Act* is, of
course, also a law of Canada although it has
a special application to Indians alone.

The judgment then refers to the case of
Regina v. Gonzales *in which a majority of the*
British Columbia Court of Appeal concluded
that Section 94 (a) of the Indian Act *does not*
abrogate or infringe the right of the appellant
and therefore the Canadian Bill of Rights *did*
not affect it. In that case, Mr. Justice Davey
wrote reasons for judgment, taking the view
that section (1) of the Bill of Rights *should be*
treated merely as providing "a canon of con-
struction for the interpretation of legislation
existing at the time when the statute was
enacted."

In writing the majority judgment of the
Supreme Court of Canada, Mr. Justice Ritchie
went on:

This proposition appears to me to strike at
the very foundations of the *Bill of Rights* and
to convert it from its apparent character as a
statutory declaration of the fundamental human rights and freedoms which it recognizes,
into being little more than a rule for the construction of federal statutes, but as this ap-
proach has found favour with some eminent
legal commentators, it seems to me to be important that priority should be given to a consideration of it.

The judgment went on to refer the 1963 case of Robertson and Rosetanni v. The Queen, *involving the* Lord's Day Act, *in which Chief Justice Cartwright disagreed with the view that the* Bill of Rights *should be regarded merely as "a canon of construction" for the interpretation of legislation. The Chief Justice had written:*

With the greatest respect, I find myself unable to agree with this view. The imperative words of the Canadian Bill of Rights *appear to me to require the courts to refuse to apply any law, coming within the legislative authority of Parliament, which infringes freedom of religion unless it is expressly declared by an Act of Parliament that the law which does so infringe shall operate notwithstanding the* Canadian Bill of Rights. *As already pointed out s. 5(2) makes it plain that the* Canadian Bill of Rights *is to apply to all laws of Canada already in existence at the time it came into force as well as to those thereafter enacted. In my opinion where there is an irreconcilable conflict between another Act of Parliament and the* Canadian Bill of Rights *the latter must prevail.*

The judgment written by Mr. Justice Ritchie then continued:

I do not find that this expression of opinion in any way conflicts with the reasoning of the majority of this Court which held that there was no conflict between the impugned section of the *Lord's Day Act* and the *Bill of Rights*. I am, however, with respect, of the opinion that Mr. Justice Davey's reasoning is untenable on another ground. The result of that reasoning is to conclude that any law of Canada which can only be "construed and applied sensibly" so that it offends against the *Bill of Rights*, is to operate notwithstanding the provisions of that Bill. I am unable to reconcile this interpretation with the opening words of s.2 where it is provided that

Every law of Canada, *unless it is express-ly declared by an Act of the Parliament of Canada that it shall operate notwithstand-ing the Canadian Bill of Rights,* be so construed and applied as not to abro-gate . . .

The italics are my own.

If Mr. Justice Davey's reasoning were correct and the *Bill of Rights* were to be construed as meaning that all laws of Canada which clearly offend the Bill were to operate notwithstanding its provisions, then the words which I have italicized in section 2 would be superfluous unless it be suggested that Parliament intended to reserve unto itself the right to exclude from the effect of the *Bill of Rights* only such statutes as are unclear in their meaning.

It seems to me that a more realistic meaning must be given to the words in question and they afford, in my view, the clearest indication that section 2 is intended to mean and does mean that if a law of Canada cannot be "sensibly construed and applied" so that it does not abrogate, abridge, or infringe one of the rights and freedoms recognized and declared by the Bill, then such law is inoperative, unless it is expressly declared by an Act of the Parliament of Canada that it shall operate notwithstanding the *Canadian Bill of Rights*.

The judgment went on to refer to the Lord's Day Act *in relation to the* Bill of Rights *as a possible infringement of freedom of religion. If freedom of religion had been circumscribed in this way, then "it would have been enough to say that 'freedom of religion' as used in the* Bill of Rights *must mean freedom of religion subject to the provisions of the* Lord's Day Act." *In the case of* Robertson and Rosetanni v. The Queen, *however, it was found that the* Lord's Day Act *and the* Bill of Rights *were not in conflict.*

166

The right which is here at issue is "the right of the individual to equality before the law and the protection of the law". Mr. Justice Tysoe, who wrote the reasons for judgment on behalf of the majority of the Court of Appeal of British Columbia in the *Gonzales Case, supra,* expressed the opinion that as these words occur in the *Bill of Rights* they mean

> A right of every person to *whom a particular law relates or extends,* no matter what may be a person's race, national origin, colour, religion or sex to stand on an equal footing with every other person to whom a particular law relates or extends and a right to the protection of the law.

With the members of the courts below, I cannot agree with this interpretation pursuant to which it seems to me that the most glaring discriminatory legislation against a racial group would have to be construed as recognizing the right of each of its individual members "to equality before the law", as long as all the other members are being discriminated against in the same way.

I think that the word "law" as used in s.1. (b) in the *Bill of Rights* is to be construed as meaning "the law of Canada" as defined in s.5(2) (i.e. Acts of the Parliament of Canada and any orders, rules or regulations thereunder) and without attempting any exhaustive definition of "equality before the law" I think that s.1(b) means at least that no individual or group of individuals is to be treated more harshly than another under that law, and I am therefore of opinion that an individual is denied equality before the law if it is made an offence punishable at law, on account of his race, for him to do something which his fellow Canadians are free to do without having committed any offence or having been made subject to any penalty.

It is only necessary for the purpose of deciding this case for me to say that in my opinion s.94(b) of the *Indian Act* is a law of Canada which creates such an offence and that it can only be construed in such manner that its application would operate so as to abrogate, abridge or infringe one of the rights declared and recognized by the *Bill of Rights*. For the reasons which I have indicated, I am therefore of opinion that s.94(b) is inoperative.

For the purpose of determining the issue raised by this appeal it is unnecessary to express any opinion respecting the operation of any other section of the *Indian Act*.

For all the above reasons I would dismiss this appeal.

Since writing the above I have had the advantage of reading the reasons for judgment prepared by the Chief Justice and by Mr. Justice Pigeon which, when read together, appear to me to lead to the conclusion that, even on the assumption that the application of the provisions of prior federal legislation has the effect of denying equality before the law, and thus discriminating against, a sector of the population "by reason of race", they must nevertheless be given full effect notwithstanding the provisions of the *Bill of Rights*. In view of this conclusion, I find it necessary to restate the position which I take in the matter.

I am in full agreement with the Chief Justice that the question here raised was not decided in the case of *Robertson and Rosetanni v. Her Majesty the Queen, supra,* and that this is the first occasion on which it has become necessary for this Court to decide it.

In my view under the provisions of section 1 of the *Bill of Rights* "the right of the individual to equality before the law" "without discrimination by reason of race" is recognized as a right which exists in Canada, and by sections 2 and 5 of that Bill it is provided that every law of Canada enacted before or after the coming into force of the Bill, unless Parliament makes an express declaration to the contrary, is to be "so construed and applied as not to abrogate, abridge, or infringe or to authorize the abroga-

tion, abridgment, or infringement" of any of
the rights so recognized and declared.

It may well be that the implementation of the
Canadian Bill of Rights by the courts can give
rise to great difficulties, but in my view full effect must be given to the terms of section 2
thereof.

The present case discloses laws of Canada
which abrogate, abridge, and infringe the right
of the individual Indian to equality before the
law and in my opinion if those laws are to be
applied in accordance with the express
language used by the Parliament in section 2 of
the *Bill of Rights,* the section 94(b) of the
Indian Act must be declared to be inoperative.

It appears to me to be desirable to make it
plain that these reasons for judgment are
limited to a situation in which, under the laws
of Canada, it is made an offence punishable at
law on account of race, for a person to do
something which all Canadians who are not
members of that race may do with impunity; in
my opinion the same considerations do not by
any means apply to all the provisions of the *Indian Act.*